Reading Comprehension Fundamentals
GRADE 4

CONTENTS

Introduction

What's in *Reading Comprehension Fundamentals*?	4
Using *Reading Comprehension Fundamentals* in Your Classroom	5
Using *Reading Comprehension Fundamentals* to Reteach and Reinforce	6

Comprehension Activities for Nonfiction Texts

Main Idea and Details	7
Text Features and Visual Information	12
Description	17
Cause and Effect	21
Compare and Contrast	26
Sequence	31
Problem and Solution	35
Vocabulary	40
Summarize	45
Predict	50
Fact and Opinion	55
Make Inferences	60
Author's Purpose	65
Text Structure	70

Nonfiction Genre Study

Expository Nonfiction	74
Persuasive Nonfiction	78
Narrative Nonfiction	82
Descriptive Nonfiction	86

CONTENTS
continued

Comprehension Activities for Fiction Texts

Character	90
Setting	95
Plot	100
Theme	105
Point of View	110
Vocabulary	115
Visual Information	119
Summarize	123
Make Inferences	127
Predict	131
Cause and Effect	135
Compare and Contrast	139
Foreshadowing	143
Idioms	147

Fiction Genre Study

Historical Fiction	151
Realistic Fiction	155
Mystery	159

Answer Key 163

What's in *Reading Comprehension Fundamentals*?

Reading Comprehension Fundamentals is your resource for reading comprehension lessons that provide the foundation for instruction and practice of reading skills and genre study. The 35 skill-based units include fiction and nonfiction texts and a variety of practice items that provide rigorous grade-level practice.

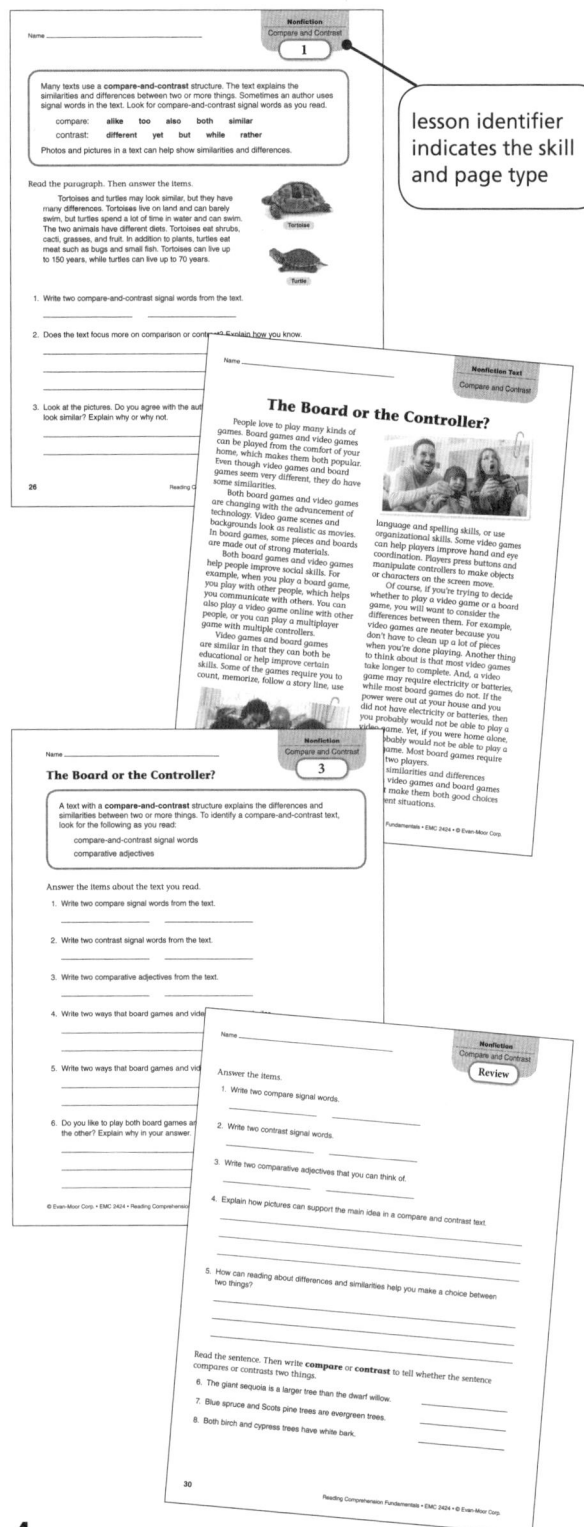

lesson identifier indicates the skill and page type

Instructional Activity Page

This page has an instructional rule box that teaches the reading comprehension skill or genre and provides a reference for students as they complete the page. Each unit has one or two instructional activity pages. There is a variety of response formats, including multiple choice, constructed response, and open-ended items.

Text Selection

The 1-page fiction and nonfiction text selections are specifically written to support each individual reading skill or genre. Nonfiction texts include science, social studies, and other real-world topics.

Text-Based Activity Page

The text-based activity page contains an instructional rule box and text-dependent items that target the reading comprehension skill or genre. The items follow various response formats, including multiple choice, constructed response, and open-ended items.

Unit Review

The review page provides an opportunity to assess students' mastery of each individual reading skill and gauge their understanding of the genre or literary element.

Using *Reading Comprehension Fundamentals* in Your Classroom

Planning Instruction
The units in this book do not need to be taught in sequential order. Choose the units that align with your curriculum or with your students' needs.

Using *Reading Comprehension Fundamentals* for Whole-Group Instruction
For whole-group instruction, introduce the unit to the whole class. Provide each student with an instructional activity page, and review the rule box as a class. Then distribute the text selection and text-based activity page. Have students read independently or in small groups. After students have read the text, have them complete the text-based activity page. Next, facilitate a class discussion based on students' responses. Encourage students to elaborate on their written responses and to engage with other students with comments and questions during the discussion.

Using *Reading Comprehension Fundamentals* for Small-Group Instruction
For small-group instruction, you may choose to assign specific units to certain groups based on student needs for targeted instruction of particular skills. Or, you may want to assign a single unit to the whole group but provide an extra instructional activity page to only a small group so that the small group can have additional instruction on that particular skill.

Using *Reading Comprehension Fundamentals* for Formative Assessment
The instructional activity pages can be used as an informal assessment of students' competencies. Student responses may inform your instruction by providing you with a detailed view of each student's level of mastery prior to assigning the unit's reading selection and text-based activity page.

Using *Reading Comprehension Fundamentals* for Summative Assessment
You may choose to use the unit review pages as formal assessments of students' mastery of specific reading comprehension skills, genres, and literary elements. The items on this page ask students to define the reading comprehension skill and to demonstrate their understanding by completing text-based items.

Using Reading Comprehension Fundamentals to Reteach and Reinforce

The perfect companion to Evan-Moor's *Daily Reading Comprehension*

Thousands of grade 1–6 teachers use *Daily Reading Comprehension* to teach reading strategies and practice reading skills. These lessons are a useful tool for informal assessment of students' skills. Student responses on the weekly *Daily Reading Comprehension* lessons will indicate the skills that need further reinforcement. Use *Reading Comprehension Fundamentals* to reteach and reinforce important reading comprehension skills and essential genre study.

For example, if a student makes errors in Week 15 Day 3 of *Daily Reading Comprehension*, your assessment is that the student needs more instruction on how to make inferences.

The student makes an incorrect inference about the text.

Use these pages from *Reading Comprehension Fundamentals* to reteach and practice skills students have not mastered.

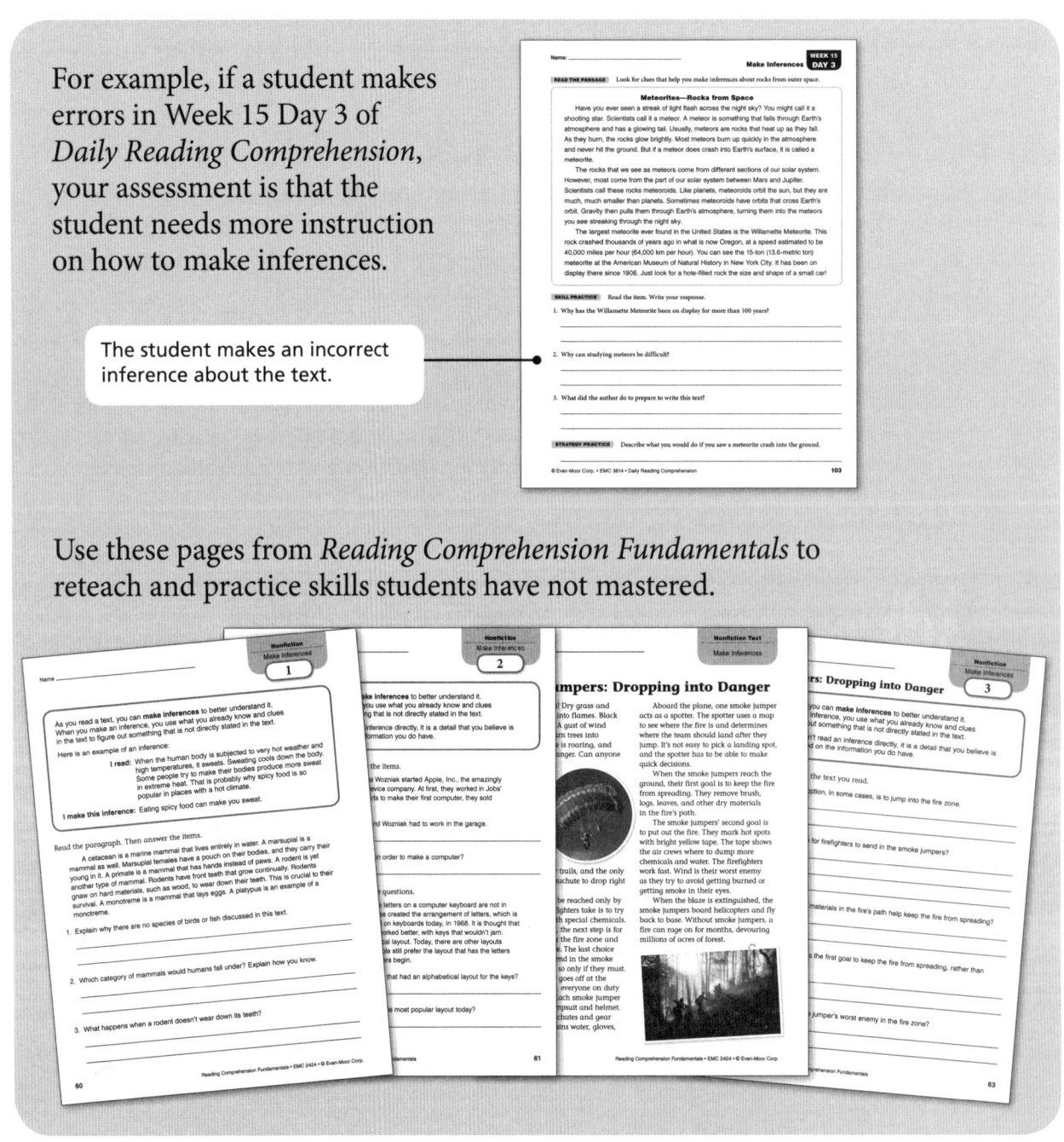

Nonfiction
Main Idea and Details

1

Name _____

In a text, the **main idea** is what the text is mostly about. Most texts explain the main idea in the first paragraph.

The rest of the text gives **supporting details**. They tell more about the main idea.

Read the main idea and each supporting detail.
Write **yes** if the detail supports the main idea.
Write **no** if the detail does not support the main idea.

Main Idea: Coconuts have many uses.	Supporting Details
No	The coconut grows on tropical palm trees.
Yes	You can chop coconut shells and mix them into garden soil to help plants grow.
No	People call the white part of the coconut *meat*.
Yes	You can drink the water in the center of the coconut's shell.
Yes	People use shredded coconut to make candy, cake, and cookies.
Yes	People use the hairy fibers from the outside of the coconut's husk to create ropes, doormats, and baskets.
No	The coconut's meat lines the inside of the hard shell.
No	It takes a year for a coconut to form and ripen.
Yes	People use coconut oil, which comes from the coconut's meat, for cooking.

Name _____

Nonfiction
Main Idea and Details

2

> The **main idea** is the most important idea in the text.
> **Supporting details** give more information about the main idea.
> Supporting details can be examples, facts, reasons, or pictures.
>
> Look for signal words and phrases when you read a text.
> These signal words and phrases often come before supporting details:
>
>   also   another   example   in addition   such as   too

Read the paragraphs. Then answer the items.

    "Ah-choo!" Sneezing is a reflex. A reflex is something that you do not choose to do, but it happens when your body reacts quickly to something. Your body uses reflexes to protect itself, and the human body has over 40 reflexes.

    Reflexes help us. For example, when you breathe in harmful germs or dust, your body makes you sneeze to get rid of the germs and dust quickly. Coughing is another reflex that helps you get germs and dust out of your body. Blinking your eyelids is also a reflex. Your eyelids close to prevent bright lights from hurting your eyes. Moving quickly is a reflex, too. If you've ever touched something very hot, you probably pulled your hand away very quickly without even thinking about it. That's because your body did not wait for your brain to decide what to do. Your body reacted quickly to protect itself when it felt the hot object.

1. What is the main idea of the text?

   Ⓐ Sneezing and coughing are important reactions.
   Ⓑ The human body uses different reflexes to protect itself.
   Ⓒ Your eyelids help you look at bright lights.
   Ⓓ You don't choose to blink, but it still happens.

2. Write four signal words or phrases from the text.

   _____   _____

   _____   _____

3. Write one sentence from the text that supports the main idea.

   _____

   _____

How We Get Salt

Salt is in our bodies, in our food, and on our kitchen tables. Salt is actually a mineral called *sodium chloride*. You probably know that salt can give your food a salty flavor. However, you may not know that people and animals need salt to live. We use salt for purposes other than flavoring food. Because we need salt, we have different ways of getting it from the earth.

Evaporation

People use evaporation to get sea salt, which we use to flavor foods. Workers find salt on seashores where the sun has dried up the water. The workers rake the salt into piles. Then they take the piles of salt to a solar evaporation plant. This is a place that has shallow pools. The workers fill the pools with the salt that they collected. Sunlight shines on these pools and makes the water evaporate until only salt crystals are left. Then the workers clean and dry the sea salt so it can be taken to stores.

Shaft Mining

In addition to getting salt from the sea, we get salt from under the ground. In some places, there is rock salt underground. Rock salt looks like rocks we see every day. To get rock salt, workers dig into the earth. They use drills to break off big pieces of salt. Then they crush it into smaller pieces. We don't eat rock salt, but we use it to soften hard water, to thaw ice on roads, and to make certain products such as soap and paper.

Solution Mining

Most of the table salt we use comes from solution mining. Solution mining is another way to get salt that's under the ground. To collect salt in this way, workers build a well over a place where there is salt underground. They fill the well with water so that it mixes with the salt. The water dissolves the salt, and the water becomes saltwater. Later, the workers use the well to bring the saltwater above ground. Then they boil the saltwater to evaporate the water, and only salt is left.

It's good that we have different ways of getting salt because we need it to live. And, most of our favorite foods wouldn't taste so good if we didn't add salt!

Name _____

Nonfiction
Main Idea and Details

3

How We Get Salt

> In a text, the **main idea** is what the text is mostly about.
> **Supporting details** give more information about the main idea.
> Supporting details can be examples, facts, descriptions, or pictures.
>
> Headings can help to organize supporting details in a text.
>
> Signal words and phrases can help you find supporting details.
>
> These are common signal words and phrases to look for as you read:
>
> also   another   for example   in addition   such as   too

Answer the items about the text you read.

1. What is the main idea of the text?
   - Ⓐ All of the salt we eat comes from a well in the ground.
   - Ⓑ Rock salt and table salt are the same thing.
   - Ⓒ There are different ways that we get salt from the earth.
   - Ⓓ Sodium chloride gives humans and animals more energy.

2. Write two signal words or phrases from the text.
   in addition   such as

3. Describe one way that we get the salt that we eat.
   workers use evaporation to get sea salt

4. Each heading tells a _____.
   - Ⓐ place where we get salt from
   - Ⓑ way to get salt that will be explained below
   - Ⓒ way to evaporate salt that will be explained below
   - Ⓓ reason why we need salt to live

5. Explain how the pictures help you understand the text better.
   th picture of a worker tells me sea salt comes from sea water

Nonfiction

Main Idea and Details

Review

Name _____

Answer the items.

1. Explain what a main idea and supporting details are.

   _____
   _____
   _____

2. Write four signal words or phrases that can help you find supporting details in a text.

   __in addition__ __such as__
   _____ _____

3. Explain how facts and examples can support a main idea.

   _____
   _____
   _____

4. Explain how a text can use pictures to support the main idea.

   _____
   _____
   _____

Read the paragraph. Then write the main idea.

5.   In cities, people rely on different kinds of transportation to go places. In most cities, people can choose to take the bus, ride in a car, ride a bike, use a skateboard, or ride a train. Some people take a ferry, or a boat, to travel around the city.

   _____
   _____
   _____

Name _____

Nonfiction
Text Features and Visual Information

1

Text features can be part of a text, a sign, or a chart. Text features tell more about the text or the topic. Text features can help an author get a message across with just a few words. These are a few kinds of text features:

  the title of the text

  bold words and headings

  pictures and captions

Read the sign. Look at the text features. Then answer the questions.

Stay Healthy by Washing Right!

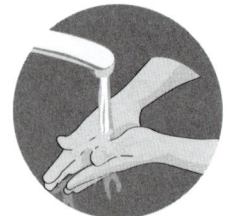 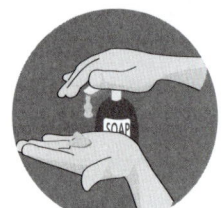 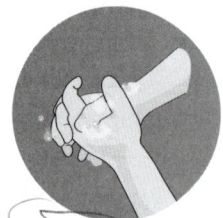 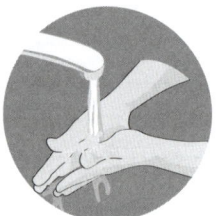 

Wet your hands with warm water. | Use soap. | Rub your hands for 20 seconds. | Rinse well with warm water. | Dry your hands with a paper towel or air dryer.

1. What conclusion can you draw from the sign's title?
   - Ⓐ You can get sick if you don't wash your hands correctly.
   - Ⓑ Your hands can get chapped if you wash them too long.
   - Ⓒ You should always dry your hands.

2. What's the best temperature for washing your hands? How do you know?
   Wash your hands with warm water

3. Do the captions help you better understand the pictures? Explain your answer.
   it would because on the 3ed step how do we know it 20 seconds

Name _____

Nonfiction
Text Features and Visual Information

2

Authors use different kinds of **visual information** in a text. Pictures, photos, graphs, and charts provide visual information.

When authors present information in a chart, do these things to help you better understand the information:

First, read the title of the chart. The title will help your mind to bring up ideas you already know about the topic.

Next, look at the column headings. Everything in one column is related to the heading.

Last, look at the rows. Everything in one row is related.

Read the chart. Then answer the items.

Number Words

	Spanish	German	English
	cero	null	zero
●	uno	eins	one
● ●	dos	zwei	two
● ● ●	tres	drei	three
● ● ● ●	quatro	veir	four
● ● ● ● ●	cinco	fünf	five

1. Write the word used for *four* in each language in the chart. How do you know the words?

   I look at top of the chart to know

2. Why do you think the author chooses to present this information in a chart?

   So we can know the numbers in spanish and German, and

Join Robotics Club!

Are you looking for something to do after school? Do you enjoy building things? Do robots interest you? Then join our Robotics Club and learn how to make your own robot. You will work in a team to build a model, write the software to operate it, and tweak it until it does exactly what you want it to do.

If you have never done anything with robots or software before, you will learn. If you already know how to build models or write programs, you can improve your skills. All club members will increase their teamwork and problem-solving skills while having a great time!

ROBOTICS Kids Club

For: Students in 4th–6th grades

When: Every Wednesday, immediately after the final bell

Where: Mr. Morningstar's Room, W72

Cost: $50 (to help cover the cost of components)

The team with the best robot will go to the **Robotics Challenge** in May!

Name _____

Nonfiction
Text Features and Visual Information

Join Robotics Club

3

> **Text features** can make important words in the text stand out.
> Look at these text features as you read:
>
>   **the title**   **bold words**   **headings**   **labels on a diagram**
>
> **Visual information** shows more about the text's topic.
> Look at the visual information as you read:
>
>   **pictures**   **photos**   **captions**   **maps**

Answer the items about the text you read.

1. Choose the **best** reason for why the author wrote this text.
   - Ⓐ to teach children how to work in a team
   - Ⓑ to keep children safe after school
   - ● to get children to join the robotics club

2. Why do you think the author put bold labels on the left side of the flyer?
   so we can easily find the info

3. Why is there a fee to join the club? How much is it?
   the fee is 50$ and help cover the cost of robot parts

4. Why do you think the author put information in a burst?
   the author wanted kids to know its a contest

© Evan-Moor Corp. • EMC 2424 • Reading Comprehension Fundamentals

Name _____

Nonfiction

Text Features and Visual Information

Review

Answer the item.

1. Mark all the examples of text features.
   Ⓐ bold words and headings
   Ⓑ problems and solutions
   Ⓒ different languages
   Ⓓ pictures and captions

Read the paragraph. Then answer the questions.

    The musical *Oklahoma!* was a big hit on Broadway in 1943. The story was about a farm girl who wonders which cowboy she should take to the picnic—and maybe marry. The writer gave the story lots of emotion, with both highs and lows. The composer wrote music that went perfectly with the lyrics. The dances were an important part of the plot.

Oklahoma! ran for 2,212 performances in New York City

2. What information did you learn from the poster?
   _____
   _____

3. What information did the caption provide? Do you think the information was important?
   _____
   _____
   _____

Name _____

Nonfiction
Description

1

> Many texts use a **description** text structure. In a text with a description structure, the author uses details and examples to support the main idea. Description texts often include pictures that provide more details about the topic.

Read the paragraph. Then answer the items.

A new style of painting called Pointillism was created in the 1800s as a result of scientific information. In the late 1800s, Georges Seurat was an artist. He read a scientific article about human vision. Scientists had discovered that the human eye blends colors that are next to each other when the eye sees them from a distance. Seurat used this fact to invent Pointillism, which is making a painting by using dots of color rather than solid strokes of color.

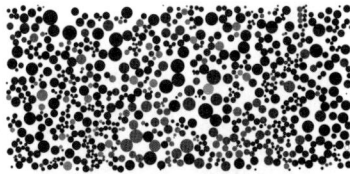
Pointillism example

Solid paint stroke

1. Write the main idea of this paragraph in your own words.

   _____
   _____

2. In your own words, write a detail from the text that supports the main idea.

   _____
   _____

3. In your own words, explain what Pointillism is.

   _____
   _____

4. Explain how the pictures help support the main idea.

   _____
   _____

The World's Fastest-Growing Plant

Bamboo is a useful plant, so it is a good thing that it grows fast. Bamboo is the tallest grass in the world. The fact that it is so tall is not surprising. It grows up to 12 inches (30.4 cm) in a single day!

Bamboo is a grass that has a thick, hollow stem that looks like a tree trunk. Because bamboo needs warmth and water, it grows in many parts of Asia and in some parts of the United States where the climate is warm and moist.

Bamboo is good for the environment because animals rely on it for food. For example, red pandas and giant pandas eat the stalks, stems, and leaves.

Even though bamboo is so useful, a mystery surrounds it. No one knows what causes bamboo to flower, so we cannot predict when a bamboo forest will flower. It could flower after 60 years or after 120 years. The problem is that animals do not eat bamboo when it flowers. And, all of the bamboo in a forest will flower at the same time. This causes the animals in that forest to go hungry. Researchers are working to solve the mystery.

People also benefit from bamboo. For instance, people eat bamboo sprouts and seeds. They feed bamboo leaves to their livestock. Bamboo is also used to build furniture and homes. Bamboo is made into high-quality paper, too. In the United States, people have bamboo flooring and kitchen countertops. Bamboo can also be made into fabric that keeps a person's body cool in summer and warm in winter. Bamboo fabric feels soft like silk, but unlike silk, it does not wrinkle and can be washed safely.

Since it grows so fast, bamboo is a renewable resource. Best of all, when an item made of bamboo is thrown out, it rots and turns into dirt over time. So, bamboo is good for the environment.

Name _____

Nonfiction
Description

2

The World's Fastest-Growing Plant

> Many texts use a **description** text structure. In a text with a description structure, the author uses details and examples to provide information about a main topic.
>
> These are description signal words and phrases:
>
> in addition   also   such as   for example   for instance

Answer the items about the text you read.

1. Write the main idea of the text.
   all the benifits of bamboo

2. Explain why bamboo is an unusual plant.
   because it can grow 12 inch a day

3. Explain why bamboo is useful to people.
   it can be used for flooring and kitchen conneertops

4. Explain why bamboo is good for the environment and for animals in the environment.
   its useful because animals rely on it for food

5. Write three description signal words or phrases from the text.
   for example   for instance   also

© Evan-Moor Corp. • EMC 2424 • Reading Comprehension Fundamentals

Name _____

Nonfiction
Description

Review

Answer the items.

1. Explain how you can identify a text with a description structure.

   _____

   _____

2. Why is it important for an author to support the main idea with details and examples?

   _____

   _____

3. Explain how pictures can help provide more details about a topic.

   _____

   _____

Read the paragraph. Then answer the items.

    There are many reasons to keep your house clean. For example, you can often prevent pests such as rodents, cockroaches, and ants from living in your home when you keep it clean. Many pests come into a home looking for food crumbs, so a house with fewer crumbs could have fewer pests. Another reason to clean is to prevent illness from germs lurking in your home. In addition, you may want to clean so that your friends enjoy spending time at your house. A clean house usually makes people feel more comfortable than a messy one does.

4. Write two description signal words or phrases from the text.

   _____   _____

5. What is the main idea of the text?

   _____

6. Write a supporting detail from the text.

   _____

   _____

Nonfiction

Cause and Effect

1

Name __10/9th/2020__

Many texts use a **cause-and-effect** structure. The text tells about an event and its result. It can also tell about something that occurred and then explain why it happened.

To find the cause, ask yourself: Why did it happen?

To find the effect, ask yourself: What was the result of _____?

Read the paragraphs. Then answer the questions.

In 1856 the United States passed the Guano Islands Act. This law said that the United States could claim an island if it met two conditions. First, the island had to have bird droppings. Second, no one could already be living there. What was the purpose of this odd law? Bird droppings, or guano, were valuable back then. Farmers used guano to fertilize crops.

The United States took over Jarvis Island in the Pacific Ocean. Workers built a dock, buildings, and a tram on it. The tram was a railroad car with a handle. A person pumped the handle up and down to make the car roll on railroad tracks.

Workers loaded the guano onto the tram. The tram rolled it to the dock. There, ships loaded the guano as cargo. For the next 20 years, the guano from Jarvis sailed to the United States. When scientists learned how to make fertilizer without bird droppings, the workers left the island.

1. Why did people build a dock and a tram on Jarvis Island?

   _____

   _____

2. What caused people to leave Jarvis Island?

   _____

   _____

3. Why was guano considered to be valuable?

   _____

   _____

Name _____

Nonfiction

Cause and Effect

2

Authors can use a **cause-and-effect** structure to help a reader understand the text. One event, or cause, can have multiple effects, or results. Example:

During a war, one country's army invades another country. People suffer.
                cause   **effect**

They do not have enough food or medical supplies. Their homes are ruined.
                              other effects

Read the paragraphs. Then answer the questions.

Audrey Hepburn was born in Belgium in 1929. Her family moved to the Netherlands. When she was 10, World War II broke out. The German army marched into the Netherlands and blocked the supply routes. Very little food entered the nation. Many people living there had barely enough food to eat. Audrey was hungry, too.

Audrey studied ballet. She wanted to be a ballerina. After the war ended in 1945, Audrey tried to join a ballet company. She was told that her bones were not strong enough because she had almost starved. Instead, she began to act in movies. Her leading role in the 1953 film *Roman Holiday* made her famous. She played many characters in films during the 1950s and 1960s.

Audrey Hepburn

1. What caused Audrey to suffer during her childhood?

    She has starving and her bones where not strong enough for ballet

2. What effect did Audrey's childhood experiences have on her career plans?

    her career was to do ballet but her bones arnt strong enough

3. What was the result of Audrey's role in *Roman Holiday*?

    it made her famous

Fire Helped Humans Thrive

Nobody knows when people began controlling fire. We do know that people have been using fire for millions of years. Its many uses helped them to survive.

In the beginning, people probably used fire for three purposes: to stay warm, to keep wild animals away, and to have light in the darkness. People built fires and stayed close to them because bears and wolves would stay away from the flames. They slept near the fire for warmth, as well.

Eventually, people discovered that roasted meat tasted good. Soon they were cooking their meats and fish. Cooking kills germs. As a result, people became sick less often.

Early people thought of more uses for fire. They burned the inner part of a log to make a dugout canoe. Using smoky torches, humans forced bees to leave their hive. This resulted in the people getting honey. They discovered that fire could be used for hunting, too. They chased large game with flaming torches until the animals plunged off cliffs. Then, by burning a smoky fire of freshly cut wood, people preserved the meat from these animals. Smoked meat did not have to be eaten right away. It lasted a long time.

Over time, people figured out that fire could heat water to boiling. This made steam, which was useful in

woodworking. It let people bend wood to form bows and baskets. It could also be used to straighten wood for spears and arrows.

People discovered that they could grow seed-bearing grasses such as wheat, oats, and rye. They needed a way to clear a field quickly so that they could plant what they wanted. It was much easier to burn a field than to cut down every bush and tree. Another good effect was that the ashes left behind improved the soil.

Once people had farms, they also built houses. Each home had a fire pit or a fireplace. Even 150 years ago a fire was always burning in most homes so that people could make soup and hot drinks at any time. Before indoor bathrooms, people used fire to heat water for their baths, too.

Today small fires burn in our homes in our gas furnaces, water heaters, stoves, dryers, and fireplaces. Thus, fire continues to help us thrive.

Nonfiction

Cause and Effect

3

Name _____

Fire Helped Humans Thrive

> A text with a **cause-and-effect structure** tells the reason something happens. A cause is something that makes an effect occur.
>
> These signal words and phrases can help you recognize cause and effect:
>
> | | | | | | |
> |---|---|---|---|---|---|
> | as a result | because | caused | consequently | due to | thus |
> | led to | resulted in | since | therefore | effect | so |

Answer the items about the text you read.

1. The text explained _____.
   - Ⓐ effects of discovering fire
   - Ⓑ causes that make fire hot
   - Ⓒ how people used grasses
   - Ⓓ why fire is not needed today

2. When people started cooking their meat, what was the effect?
   people became sick less often

3. In the third paragraph, what signal words did the author use to explain why early people started cooking meat and getting sick less often?
   as a result   _effect_

4. Finish the sentence using a cause-and-effect signal word.

   The use of flaming torches in hunting ____caused____ many animals' deaths.

24   Reading Comprehension Fundamentals • EMC 2424 • © Evan-Moor Corp.

Name _____

Nonfiction
Cause and Effect

Review

Mark the sentence that shows a cause-and-effect relationship.

1. Ⓐ The sun gives off heat and light.
   Ⓑ The heat from the sun can burn your skin.
   Ⓒ The sun shines only during the summer.
   Ⓓ The sun's heat is different every day.

Write four cause-and-effect signal words or phrases.

2. _____   _____

   _____   _____

Read the sentence. Underline the **cause**. Circle the **effect**.

3. Eating too much sugar is bad for your teeth.

4. People who laugh a lot are generally happier.

5. Wind and rain cause rocks to erode.

6. Hanging your clothes to dry outside saves energy.

Answer the item.

7. Why might an author use a cause-and-effect structure to explain something?

   _____

   _____

Read the sentence. Then write the cause-and-effect relationship it tells about.

8. Some people like to record television shows so they can skip the commercials.

   _____

   _____

   _____

Name _____

Nonfiction
Compare and Contrast

1

Many texts use a **compare-and-contrast** structure. The text explains the similarities and differences between two or more things. Sometimes an author uses signal words in the text. Look for compare-and-contrast signal words as you read.

compare: **alike   too   also   both   similar**

contrast: **different   yet   but   while   rather**

Photos and pictures in a text can help show similarities and differences.

Read the paragraph. Then answer the items.

Tortoises and turtles may look similar, but they have many differences. Tortoises live on land and can barely swim, but turtles spend a lot of time in water and can swim. The two animals have different diets. Tortoises eat shrubs, cacti, grasses, and fruit. In addition to plants, turtles eat meat such as bugs and small fish. Tortoises can live up to 150 years, while turtles can live up to 70 years.

Tortoise

Turtle

1. Write two compare-and-contrast signal words from the text.

   _____   _____

2. Does the text focus more on comparison or contrast? Explain how you know.

   _____

   _____

   _____

3. Look at the pictures. Do you agree with the author's statement that tortoises and turtles look similar? Explain why or why not.

   _____

   _____

26   Reading Comprehension Fundamentals • EMC 2424 • © Evan-Moor Corp.

Name _____

Nonfiction
Compare and Contrast

2

A text with a **compare-and-contrast** structure explains the similarities and differences between two or more things. A compare-and-contrast text often uses comparative adjectives.

These are examples of comparative adjectives:

| longer | more athletic | less cheerful | healthier | smarter |
| calmer | more beautiful | less talkative | slower | |

Read the sentence. Then write **compare** or **contrast** to tell whether the sentence compares or contrasts two things.

1. Traveling by airplane is faster than traveling by ship. _____

2. Trains and airplanes both offer comfortable ways to travel. _____

3. The bus is less comfortable than the train. _____

4. Traveling in a train car is often more luxurious than driving your own car. _____

Read the paragraph. Then answer the items.

    In many cities, you can travel by ferry or by train. On both, there is room to walk around, and there is seating. A ferry is usually more spacious than a train, though. Most ferries have at least two levels, but most city trains have only one level. Taking the train is obviously more convenient for most people because more people ride trains than ferries. The ferry provides an important transportation service to people who live and work in cities, and the train system does, too.

5. Write two comparative adjectives from the text.

_____   _____

6. Write one way that ferries and trains are different and one way they are the same.

_____

_____

© Evan-Moor Corp. • EMC 2424 • Reading Comprehension Fundamentals

The Board or the Controller?

People love to play many kinds of games. Board games and video games can be played from the comfort of your home, which makes them both popular. Even though video games and board games seem very different, they do have some similarities.

Both board games and video games are changing with the advancement of technology. Video game scenes and backgrounds look as realistic as movies. In board games, some pieces and boards are made out of strong materials.

Both board games and video games help people improve social skills. For example, when you play a board game, you play with other people, which helps you communicate with others. You can also play a video game online with other people, or you can play a multiplayer game with multiple controllers.

Video games and board games are similar in that they can both be educational or help improve certain skills. Some of the games require you to count, memorize, follow a story line, use

language and spelling skills, or use organizational skills. Some video games can help players improve hand and eye coordination. Players press buttons and manipulate controllers to make objects or characters on the screen move.

Of course, if you're trying to decide whether to play a video game or a board game, you will want to consider the differences between them. For example, video games are neater because you don't have to clean up a lot of pieces when you're done playing. Another thing to think about is that most video games take longer to complete. And, a video game may require electricity or batteries, while most board games do not. If the power were out at your house and you did not have electricity or batteries, then you probably would not be able to play a video game. Yet, if you were home alone, you probably would not be able to play a board game. Most board games require at least two players.

The similarities and differences between video games and board games are what make them both good choices for different situations.

Name _____

Nonfiction
Compare and Contrast

The Board or the Controller?

3

> A text with a **compare-and-contrast** structure explains the differences and similarities between two or more things. To identify a compare-and-contrast text, look for the following as you read:
>
>   compare-and-contrast signal words
>
>   comparative adjectives

Answer the items about the text you read.

1. Write two compare signal words from the text.

   _____   _____

2. Write two contrast signal words from the text.

   _____   _____

3. Write two comparative adjectives from the text.

   _____   _____

4. Write two ways that board games and video games are similar.

   _____

   _____

5. Write two ways that board games and video games are different.

   _____

   _____

6. Do you like to play both board games and video games? Or, do you prefer to play one or the other? Explain why in your answer.

   _____

   _____

   _____

© Evan-Moor Corp. • EMC 2424 • Reading Comprehension Fundamentals

Name _____

Nonfiction
Compare and Contrast

Review

Answer the items.

1. Write two compare signal words.

   _____   _____

2. Write two contrast signal words.

   _____   _____

3. Write two comparative adjectives that you can think of.

   _____   _____

4. Explain how pictures can support the main idea in a compare and contrast text.

   _____

   _____

   _____

5. How can reading about differences and similarities help you make a choice between two things?

   _____

   _____

   _____

Read the sentence. Then write **compare** or **contrast** to tell whether the sentence compares or contrasts two things.

6. The giant sequoia is a larger tree than the dwarf willow.   _____

7. Blue spruce and Scots pine trees are evergreen trees.   _____

8. Both birch and cypress trees have white bark.   _____

Name _____

Nonfiction
Sequence

1

> **Text structure** is the way an author gives information.
>
> **Sequence** is the order of events in a text. Signal words in the text can help you know the order in which things happened.
>
> Look for signal words that help tell about sequence:
>
> | after | before | next | then | later |
> |---|---|---|---|---|
> | finally | first | second | last | |

Read the paragraph. Then answer the items.

  Dr. Samuel Gridley Howe ran the Perkins School for the Blind in Massachusetts. Laura Bridgman was a blind and deaf girl who could not speak. In 1836, when Laura was 7 years old, Dr. Howe designed a way to teach her the words for familiar items such as a fork and a broom. First, on each item, he glued its name in raised print and had her feel the words. Next, he removed the labels and had Laura match the labels to the items. Then, he cut apart the raised letters. Later, she put the letters together to form the words. In this way, Dr. Howe taught her all the letters of the alphabet and the numerals. Finally, he held her hand and showed her how to form each letter with a pencil. In less than two years, Laura could write her name! She became the first deaf-blind person in history who learned to read and write.

1. Underline the sequence signal words in the text. Write them on the line.

   _____

2. When did Dr. Howe cut apart the letters? Why did he do it?

   _____

   _____

   _____

3. What was the last step in the process? Why do you think it was the last step?

   _____

   _____

Hattie McDaniel, Academy Award-Winning Actor

Hattie McDaniel was born in 1895 in Kansas. She was the youngest of 13 children. From an early age, she showed remarkable singing and acting talent. She left school when she was just 15 to sing in a traveling show. In 1925 she became one of the first African American women to sing on the radio in the United States. At that time, performers sang live on the air. Every day at a certain time, Hattie would sing, and people would tune in to hear her.

In the early 1930s the Great Depression was a time of hardship for almost everyone in America. It ended Hattie's radio career. She took work as a bathroom attendant in a Wisconsin club called Club Madrid. She sang as she worked. The club's customers noticed her beautiful voice. They asked the owner to let her sing on stage. She sang at Club Madrid for a year. Then her brother called to say that he had found her a spot on a radio show in Los Angeles. On this show, Hattie didn't sing. She played a character in a drama, which was a radio play. During this time there were no televisions. A radio drama was like a TV show without the images. The story was told through the characters' conversations. Sound effects also helped listeners to imagine the action.

Back then, people only saw movies in theaters. Movies were just starting to become popular. Like many other radio performers, Hattie tried out for movie roles. She played small parts in more than 40 films during the 1930s. Then she was offered the role of Mammy in *Gone With the Wind*. This 1939 movie was a box-office hit. It made the most money of any film up to that time. It is considered one of the most successful films of all time.

In 1940 Hattie became the first African American to win an Academy Award. She received the Academy Award for Best Supporting Actor for her role as Mammy. During World War II, Hattie sang for the American troops fighting overseas. Then, in 1951 she worked for the first time on a TV show. Sadly, she found out that she had cancer and died in 1952. However, her memory lives on today, and two stars on the Hollywood Walk of Fame honor her.

Name _____

Nonfiction
Sequence

2

Hattie McDaniel

> A biography always has a **sequence**, or time order, text structure. It tells about a real person's life. It gives the main events in the person's life in the order in which they happened.
>
> Sometimes a biography starts by telling the reader the most important thing the person did. Then the author goes back and explains the life events leading up to it.

Answer the questions about the text you read.

1. Which of these events happened first?
   - Ⓐ Hattie sang on the radio.
   - Ⓑ Hattie played a character in a radio drama.
   - Ⓒ Hattie sang at Club Madrid.
   - Ⓓ Hattie played Mammy in *Gone With the Wind*.

2. What was Hattie's success in 1940?

   _____

   _____

3. How did entertainment change during Hattie's lifetime?

   _____

   _____

   _____

   _____

4. Do you think the sequence structure worked well for telling Hattie McDaniel's story? Explain your answer.

   _____

   _____

© Evan-Moor Corp. • EMC 2424 • Reading Comprehension Fundamentals

Name _____

Nonfiction
Sequence

Review

Answer the items.

1. What is text structure?

   _____

   _____

2. Finish the sentence.

   A sequence text structure tells _____.

3. Write four sequence signal words.

   _____   _____

   _____   _____

4. Why is the sequence text structure important in a biography?

   _____

   _____

Read the paragraph. Then answer the questions.

   Ludwig van Beethoven was a famous German composer. He was born in 1770 in Bonn and began learning the piano when he was only four. He also learned to play the violin. Beethoven visited Vienna, which was a very musical city, in 1787. Two other famous composers lived in Vienna at that time. Wolfgang Mozart and Joseph Haydn met Beethoven and gave his music high praise. Beethoven made friends in Vienna and returned there in 1792. He studied music with Haydn and lived in Vienna for the rest of his life.

5. Does this paragraph use a sequence text structure? Tell how you know.

   _____

   _____

6. Should this paragraph have used sequence signal words? Explain your answer.

   _____

Name _____ 11/3rd

Nonfiction

Problem and Solution

1

An author may use a **problem-and-solution** text structure to give the reader information. In a problem-and-solution text, the author states a problem. Then the author provides solutions, or ways to fix the problem.

The author may also provide background information about the topic to let readers know why they should care about the problem.

Read the paragraph. Then answer the items.

Human activity may be causing climate change by releasing too much carbon dioxide into the air. But it doesn't need to be this way. You can reduce your carbon footprint, or how much carbon dioxide you put into the air, and it isn't even that hard to do. It's all about saving energy. Recycling saves energy. Recycling paper takes much less energy than cutting down a tree to make paper from raw wood. Recycling also reduces the number of trees that are cut down. The more trees there are, the more carbon dioxide they can remove from the air we breathe. Recycle everything you can! Turn off the lights when you leave a room. Run your air conditioner on low. Together, we can fight climate change!

1. What is the problem in the text?

    people are putting too much carbon dioxid in the air

2. Write three solutions given in the text.

    recycleing saves energy
    turn off lights when leaving a room

3. Why do you think the author stated the problem in the first sentence?

    so the reader can know its very importand tr save energy

Name _____

Nonfiction
Problem and Solution

2

An author may use a **problem-and-solution** text structure to give the reader information. In a problem-and-solution text, the author states a problem. Then the author provides solutions, or ways to fix the problem.

The author may also provide background information about the topic to let readers know why they should care about the problem.

Read the paragraph. Then answer the questions.

Some people are born with red-green colorblindness. That means that they see normally but can't distinguish between red and green. This causes problems for them with traffic lights. They also can't tell when bananas are ripe (green bananas look the same to them as yellow ones) or tell ketchup apart from chocolate sauce. Recently, scientists made special glasses called EnChroma™. The lenses in these glasses have special filters. Wearing them helps color-blind people see the difference between red and green. They cannot see these colors as well as people without colorblindness. But the fact that they can see the difference is a great start.

1. What is the problem for people born with red-green colorblindness?
   Ⓐ They can't see anything clearly.
   Ⓑ They can't see blue lettering on a yellow shirt.
   Ⓒ They can't see the difference between red and green.
   Ⓓ They can't see things that are far away.

2. Is there a solution to the problem? If so, write about it.

   _____
   _____

3. Did the author provide information that made you care about the problem? Explain your answer.

   _____
   _____
   _____
   _____

Preventing Floods

When a rainy weather system moves over an area, its clouds are loaded with moisture. They may dump rain so fast or for so long that the ground gets soaked. It cannot absorb any more water. The extra water runs off the land and flows into lakes, streams, and rivers. Streams and rivers may not be able to carry so much water. They spill over their banks, causing a flood. Flooding is the most common natural disaster in the United States.

When a river overflows, its water spreads out, sometimes for miles. It covers roads, making them unpassable. The floodwaters pick up anything in the way and carry it along. The dirty, murky water can destroy bridges, cars, homes, businesses, and farms. People and animals are in danger of drowning.

A flood may leave many people homeless. And even if their houses are not ruined, everything the water touched may be wrecked. That means they must replace furniture, floors, and clothes. It costs a lot to recover from a flood.

The U.S. government has taken action to reduce flooding. It has built dams to protect places that often flood. A concrete dam is very tall and blocks a river valley. During heavy rains, the river water collects behind the dam, rising higher and higher. Gates beneath the dam allow just some of the water to pass through. These dams have prevented or reduced the damage caused by floods.

There are things you can do to reduce flooding, too. If you see litter, leaves, or branches clogging street gutters, pick them up and throw them out. When the gutters are blocked, rainwater cannot drain away. Blocked gutters can cause flooded streets and basements. If you have a yard, plant trees, bushes, and flowers. The plants' roots help absorb water. When there is a flood watch, you can volunteer to help others place sandbags along riverbanks. This raises the banks of the river to keep its water from spilling into streets and homes.

There is no way to prevent every flood. Fortunately when weather experts see that there may be a flood, they issue alerts on the radio, TV, and cell phones. They tell people where to go for free, safe shelter. Nobody can control the weather. So it's good to know that there are plans in place to keep us safe when there's just too much rain.

Name _____

Nonfiction
Problem and Solution

3

Preventing Floods

> An author may use a **problem-and-solution** text structure to give the reader information. In a problem-and-solution text, the author states a problem. Then the author provides solutions, or ways to fix the problem.
>
> The author may also provide background information about the topic to let readers know why they should care about the problem.

Answer the items about the text you read.

1. Does the title state the problem? Explain your answer.

   _____
   _____
   _____

2. Write two problems related to flooding that are stated in the text.

   _____
   _____
   _____

3. Write two solutions that are presented in the text.

   _____
   _____
   _____

4. Does the author provide information that makes you care about the problem? Explain your answer.

   _____
   _____
   _____

Name _____

Nonfiction
Problem and Solution

Review

Answer the items.

1. Explain what a problem-and-solution text structure is.

   _____
   _____
   _____

2. What does an author do to make you care about the problem?

   _____
   _____

3. Do you think a problem-and-solution text structure is a good way to give a reader information? Explain your answer.

   _____
   _____
   _____
   _____

Read the paragraph. Then answer the questions.

   Most of the fresh vegetables we eat grow in agricultural fields across the United States. Sometimes pests start to eat the vegetables before they are harvested. If this happens, the vegetables cannot be sold to grocery stores.

4. Is this a problem-and-solution text? Explain your answer.

   _____
   _____

5. Does the paragraph provide enough background information about the problem? Explain your answer.

   _____
   _____

Name _____

Nonfiction
Vocabulary

1

11/29

When you read, you may come across unfamiliar **vocabulary**, or words, that you don't know. When you come to a word you don't know the meaning of, try this:

Look at the surrounding words. Think about what would make sense in the sentence.

Think about what you already know about the topic.

Read the sentence before the word. Read the sentence after the word.

Read the paragraph. Then answer the items.

The Hybrid Assistive Limb (HAL) is a robotic suit. A woman wearing a HAL can lift five times more than she can lift alone. HAL 3 covers just a person's legs. HAL 5 is a full-body suit. It covers a person's legs, arms, and torso. HAL is used for physically taxing jobs. Hospital workers who wear a HAL can lift patients without hurting their own backs. Rescue workers who wear a HAL can lift heavy pieces of debris to find survivors after an earthquake. A HAL can also help people with disabilities to walk and to rise from a seated position.

1. From information in the text, the word *taxing* probably means _____.
   - Ⓐ difficult
   - Ⓑ costly
   - Ⓒ simple
   - Ⓓ expensive

2. Using information from the text, explain what the word *debris* means. Tell how you know.
   the remains of something broken down because after a earthquake there will be stuff broken down

3. What is a *torso*? Tell how you used clues in the text to figure it out.
   the trunk of something it says it covers the legs and arms of something

Name _____

Nonfiction

Vocabulary

2

When you read, you may come across unfamiliar **vocabulary**, or words, that you don't know. You can use information in the text to help you figure out a word's meaning. Check to see if the author provided a clue by using the following:

a definition in the sentence before or after the word

a word that has the same meaning

a word that has the opposite meaning

Read the paragraph. Then answer the items.

Senegal is an African nation. It has a bright pink lake! Lake Retba looks like it's full of strawberry milk, and its shore is covered by big white salt lumps. This odd lake is completely natural. A huge amount of single-celled algae is what causes the unusual coloration. When the lake's water evaporates during droughts, the concentration of algae is so high that the water turns red. Lake Retba is a saline lake. Its water has ten times more salt than the oceans. People easily float in the lake because the saltwater makes them buoyant. They can't sink. However, the water is so salty that it can damage human skin. Before diving in, people are advised to rub on a thick layer of shea butter.

1. From information in the text, the word *saline* probably means _____.
   - Ⓐ cold
   - Ⓑ pink
   - ● salty
   - Ⓓ colorful

2. What word could the author have used instead of *advised*?
   The author could use the word suggested

3. Write the word that the author defined in the text. Then write the sentence that gave the definition. Use quotation marks for the definition.
   The author defined saline because "its water was 10 times more salt"

© Evan-Moor Corp. • EMC 2424 • Reading Comprehension Fundamentals

41

Smarty Jones, Champion Thoroughbred

Smarty Jones is a champion thoroughbred whose racing ability amazed fans worldwide. Smarty was born in 2001 and was reared at the Someday Farm in Pennsylvania. His owners, Roy and Pat Chapman, knew there was something special about this young colt.

In July 2003, when Smarty Jones was two and a half years old, he suffered a bad injury. Before he had ever run in a race, his trainers were teaching him how to get set in the starting gate. Smarty did not want to stay in place. He reared up on his hind legs and smashed his head against the iron bars of the starting gate. Smarty fell to the ground unconscious. He lay bleeding in the dirt with his left eye swollen shut. His trainer thought he was dead.

Smarty was rushed to a veterinarian. Fortunately, the breaks in his skull were small fractures, and the bones in his eye socket would heal. After three weeks in the hospital, Smarty went home. In November 2003, Smarty made his racing debut and won a small local race. He won by seven and three-quarters lengths. Two weeks later, he won again, this time by 15 lengths.

Smarty's owners and trainers thought he might be a champion. In May 2004, they entered him in the famous Kentucky Derby. Smarty raced to victory with a time of 2 minutes and 4.06 seconds.

Then, on May 15, Smarty Jones won the Preakness Stakes by eleven and a half lengths! No horse had ever won by such a long distance. His jockey, Stewart Elliot, thought Smarty could win the Triple Crown.

The Triple Crown is a series of three famous races. The first race is the Kentucky Derby. It is 1 1/4 miles long. The second race is the Preakness Stakes. It is 1 3/16 miles long. The third is the Belmont Stakes. At 1 1/2 miles, it is the longest race. Smarty came in second at Belmont. But he was still a winner. Only 12 horses have ever won all three races in the Triple Crown.

Smarty injured his ankles and did not race again. But his owners began breeding him, and his first foals were born in 2006. Beginning in 2008, the Smarty Jones Stakes has been held in Arkansas every January.

Name _____

Nonfiction
Vocabulary

3

Smarty Jones, Champion Thoroughbred

> When you read, you may come across unfamiliar **vocabulary**, or words, that you don't know. You can use information in the text to help you figure out a word's meaning. Check to see if the author provided a clue by using the following:
>
> - a definition in the sentence before or after the word
> - a word that has the same meaning
> - a word than has the opposite meaning

Answer the items about the text you read.

1. From the information in the text, the word *unconscious* probably means _____.
   - Ⓐ moaning
   - Ⓑ asleep
   - Ⓒ confused
   - Ⓓ smiling

2. Using information from the text, explain what the word *debut* means. Tell how you know.
   _____
   _____
   _____

3. Using information from the text, explain what the word *fractures* means. Tell how you know.
   _____
   _____
   _____

4. Write a definition for the word *foals*. Then write the clues from the text.
   _____
   _____

© Evan-Moor Corp. • EMC 2424 • Reading Comprehension Fundamentals 43

Name _____

Nonfiction

Vocabulary

Review

Read the pair of sentences. Then answer the item.

1. You can see how symmetry is used as a way to organize a building. A house might have the same number of rooms on the left and right sides, for example.

   The word *symmetry* probably means:

   Ⓐ colors that are alike
   Ⓑ walls that are curved
   Ⓒ two sides that are the same
   Ⓓ two sides that are different

Answer the item.

2. Write two things you can do if you come across an unfamiliar word.

   _____

   _____

   _____

Read the paragraph. Then answer the items.

   Writing music is like writing stories. A person who writes music is known as a composer. A composer thinks of a musical idea and writes it on paper for others to read. Instead of writing words, a composer uses musical notation. Other people can read the notes and play them. When they do, they're playing music that came from the composer's imagination.

3. Using information in the text, explain what *musical notation* probably means.

   _____

   _____

4. Write the sentences that helped you figure it out. Use quotation marks.

   _____

   _____

   _____

Name _____

Nonfiction
Summarize

1

When you **summarize** a text, you state the text's most important ideas in your own words. Do these things to write a summary:

Write the main idea for each paragraph.

Write answers to these questions about the text:

Who/What?   Did what?   Where?   Why?   When?   How?

Read the paragraph. Then complete the graphic organizer.

> Edgar Degas was a famous artist who lived in the late 1800s. He was a perfectionist who thought his paintings were never good enough. Degas spent years on each painting. He did some parts over and over. In his *Dancers at the Barre*, he changed the dancers' legs eight times. Even after he sold a piece of art, he would visit its owner. He would snatch the painting from the wall and leave. Then he'd work on improving it.

Question	Answer
Who/What?	
Did what?	
When?	
Where?	
Why?	
How?	
Summary:	

© Evan-Moor Corp. • EMC 2424 • Reading Comprehension Fundamentals

Name _____

Nonfiction
Summarize

2

When you **summarize** a text, you state the text's most important ideas in your own words.

First, find the main idea for each paragraph. It may be stated, or you may have to use context clues to determine what it is.

To determine the main idea, decide what is most important, and write it in one or two sentences.

Next, put each of the main idea sentences together. These sentences form your summary.

Read the paragraphs. Then answer the items.

More than 2,000 years ago, the Nabataean people carved the city of Petra into stone cliffs. The cliffs stood in a desert in the Middle East. However, the people left no records about their tools or building techniques. We do not know how they cut the city into the rock.

Petra was a busy place. More than 30,000 people lived there. When an earthquake struck in 363 CE, most of the people left. In 551 CE, another huge earthquake buried the city beneath the sand.

For centuries, Petra lay hidden. In 1812, a Swiss explorer found it. Today, over 800 of the carved buildings have been unearthed. Archaeologists think that 95 percent of Petra is still buried. They continue digging to uncover this fascinating city.

1. Write the main idea of the second paragraph in one or two sentences.

_____

_____

_____

2. Write the main idea of the third paragraph in one or two sentences.

_____

_____

_____

Yo-Yo Ma, Extraordinary Musician

Yo-Yo Ma is a Chinese American cellist. He is famous because he is an extraordinary musician. He has also helped many people to get interested in the music of different cultures.

Ma was born in 1955 in Paris, France. He was a child prodigy. That means that at the age of 5, he was playing the cello as if he were a highly trained adult! His parents saw how special he was. They moved to New York City. There he performed at Carnegie Hall. He was just 9 years old. Carnegie Hall is one of the best-known concert halls in the world. Only the most talented musicians and orchestras play there.

A famous music teacher named Leonard Rose tutored Ma. Then Ma went to the Juilliard School. Only 7 out of 100 people who apply get accepted. By the time he was ready for college, orchestras around the world were asking Ma to play with them. He decided to go to college.

He went to Harvard University. College was hard. In just his first year, Ma played 30 concerts around the world. At the same time, he earned good grades. The year after he graduated from college, he won the Avery Fisher Prize. It is the highest honor for an American musician. Ma played in many orchestras and made dozens of albums. Over the years, he earned 18 Grammy Awards. A musician receives this award for outstanding achievement.

Yo-Yo Ma

Ma wanted to help people from all cultures learn to celebrate their differences. He traveled around the world. He taught himself to play the instruments of Asia, Africa, and South America. In 1998 he began the Silk Road Project. It brings together people and ideas from around the world. Musicians from different cultures work together. They blend their styles as they write and play music.

In 2011 Ma was given the Presidential Medal of Freedom. This is the highest honor the U.S. government can give to one of its citizens. Ma received it for promoting world peace and cultural understanding. In that same year Ma was awarded a Kennedy Center Honor. It is given to performers who have made important contributions to American culture.

Name _____

Nonfiction
Summarize

3

Yo-Yo Ma, Extraordinary Musician

When you **summarize** a text, you retell the text's most important ideas in your own words. In a biography, important information is written throughout the text. Do these things to write a summary of a biography:

Write about the most important events in each period of the person's life.

Write about the person's most important accomplishments.

Complete the graphic organizer with information from the text you read.

1.

Yo-Yo Ma	Most Important Information
Early years	
Education	
Silk Road Project	
Awards	

Use the information from the graphic organizer to write a summary of the text.

2. _____
_____
_____
_____

48   Reading Comprehension Fundamentals • EMC 2424 • © Evan-Moor Corp.

Name _____

Nonfiction
Summarize

Review

Answer the items.

1. When I summarize a text, I _____.
   - Ⓐ retell important information from the first paragraph
   - Ⓑ ask and answer questions about the author
   - Ⓒ write my opinion about the text
   - Ⓓ retell the text's most important ideas

2. Write the six questions you can ask yourself when you write a summary.

   _____   _____

   _____   _____

   _____   _____

3. Why is a summary always shorter than the text it summarizes?

   _____

   _____

4. Is a summary helpful to someone who has not read the text? Explain your answer.

   _____

   _____

Read the paragraph. Then write a summary of the paragraph.

5.   Alfred Wegener was a scientist who worked during the early 1900s. He came up with an unusual theory about Earth. Wegener thought that Earth's seven continents had not always existed. His theory stated that 250 million years ago there was only one giant continent. He called the super continent Pangaea. He theorized that Pangaea changed over millions of years and started breaking up. The pieces of land slowly drifted apart, becoming the seven continents we know today.

   _____

   _____

   _____

   _____

Name _____

Nonfiction
Predict

1

When you **predict**, you think of what will happen next. You can predict as you read. Use what you read and what you know to predict what will happen next.

I read: People in the Northern United States experience cold winters almost every year. For people who have certain health conditions, such as arthritis, the cold weather has serious affects on their health. Each year, more states are experiencing increasingly colder winter temperatures. Many doctors agree that cold weather can be hard on the body. Some doctors advise their patients to go to a warmer climate during winter, if possible, to ease their pain.

I know: Many people go to Florida for the winter because it has warm weather.

I predict: The number of people who go to Florida this winter will be higher than the number of people who went there last year.

Read the paragraph. Then answer the items.

You are watching a TV show and see a woman running along a river. Suddenly, she shrieks and starts to sink into the ground! The more she thrashes her arms and legs, the deeper she sinks. What is going on? The woman stepped into quicksand. It forms when sand has a lot of water in it. It looks solid but acts like a liquid. Television shows make it look as if people drown in quicksand. Yet it is very rare that quicksand is more than 3 feet deep. If you step into quicksand, stay calm. Struggling will make you sink. Slowly move your arms and feet apart. Lie on your back. Your body will float, just like in water. Swim to the edge of the quicksand. Grab a tree branch or thick root and pull yourself out.

1. A man steps into quicksand. Predict what will happen if he does not act calm.

   he will drown and die because hes dose not act calm

2. Predict what will happen if an area of sand by a pond gets flooded.

   it will turn in to quick sand.

Nonfiction
Predict

2

Name _____

> When you **predict**, you think of what will probably happen next.
>
> As you read farther in the text, your prediction will often be correct. But it may also be incorrect. That's okay. Sometimes an author wants to surprise you.
>
> What is important is that you think about the text and consider what is likely to happen.

Read each text excerpt. Write a prediction. Then see if your prediction comes true.

In June 2011, people were shocked when an emperor penguin appeared on Peka Peka Beach in New Zealand. These penguins live in Antarctica.

1. I predict that _the penguin belonged at antartica_

Scientists did not want to interfere. So they watched the penguin. The penguin did not look for food. He stayed on the beach eating sand.

2. I predict that _the sand mad him very ill_

Eating sand made the penguin very ill. Zoo workers picked him up and took him to the zoo. They put him into icy cold water and fed him krill and squid. They named him Happy Feet.

3. I predict that _he thought the sand was snow_

Scientists think he ate the sand because penguins eat snow to get fresh water. Happy Feet had an operation to remove the sand from his belly. It took him 9 weeks to recover.

4. I predict that _Happy feet went home_

In September 2011 a ship carried the head zoo keeper and Happy Feet almost 2,000 miles. Antarctica is surrounded by ice floes, so the ship couldn't get any closer.

5. I predict that _Happ feet made it home_

No one knows for certain whether Happy Feet made it home. The transmitter he had on fell off shortly after he was released.

Having Fun with Sand Dunes

Great Sand Dunes National Park in Colorado features the tallest sand dunes in the United States. People looked at those sand dunes and thought, "What could I do for fun here?" The answer is sandboarding. It looks like surfing or snowboarding, but it's done on sand dunes. It requires a special sandboard. During summer months, people can only board in the evening or early morning because the sand's surface can reach 150°F (65.56°C) in the sun.

How does a person learn sandboarding? It's a matter of trial and error. The best way to learn is to get out there and try it. Most people rent a sandboard. It has a waxed base and two bindings. The bindings attach to the rider's bare feet or footwear. These bindings make the board more like a snowboard than a surfboard. Choosing a steep dune is important, and the sand must be absolutely dry.

Great Sand Dunes National Park allows sandboarding on dunes that do not have plant life. That's because vegetation in sandy places is fragile. It's also necessary to hold the sand in place and keep it from blowing away.

If a person gets bored sandboarding in the United States, there are even taller sand dunes in Chile and Australia. The Sahara Desert in Africa has the tallest dunes in the world. They can be more than a quarter mile high.

For those who lack the balancing skills needed for sandboarding, there is sand sledding. A snow sled won't work on sand. Instead, a special sand sled is used that has a very slick bottom. It takes thrill seekers rocketing to the base of the dune.

What's the drawback to sandboarding and sand sledding? Getting back up the dune to go down again! Walking up a steep sand slope takes effort. The loose sand fills a climber's shoes, making them heavy. The person must use extra energy to make each step. Walking barefoot is easier, but it is still more tiring than walking on a hard surface.

Name __11/15__

Having Fun with Sand Dunes

Nonfiction
Predict

3

> When you **predict**, you think of what will probably happen next. You can predict as you read. Use what you read and what you know to make predictions.
>
> You can make predictions about what the text will be about.
>
> You can make predictions about what will happen next.
>
> You can make predictions about what might happen in a certain situation.

Answer the items about the text you read.

1. Based on the title, what might a person predict the text will be about?
   sand Dunes

2. Predict what would happen if a person did not use the bindings on the sandboard.
   the person it will fall of the board

3. What do you think will happen if a person sandboards on a dune that has plant life?
   vegetation in sanky places is fragile

4. Predict what would happen if a person went sandboarding in the middle of the day in Great Sand Dunes National Park during summer?
   great sand dunes natinal pa the persen will get burned

5. The best sandboarder in the world is looking for a place to hold a competition. Where do you think the competition will be held? Explain your answer.
   great sand dunes natihal park

Name _____

Nonfiction

Predict

Review

Answer the items.

1. Write two things that you can make predictions about as you read a text.

   _____
   _____
   _____

2. Explain why you must think very carefully about a text's details in order to make a prediction.

   _____
   _____
   _____

Read the paragraph. Then answer the items.

    Scorpions are nocturnal predators that will eat just about anything, including other scorpions. When a scorpion grabs another creature, it stings the creature multiple times. Scorpions are built to survive. They have strong, durable bodies, and they can live for up to a year with no food. Scorpions are known for being extremely aggressive, even towards creatures that are much larger than they are.

3. Make a prediction for when you are most likely to encounter an aggressive scorpion.
   - Ⓐ in the middle of the night
   - Ⓑ in the afternoon
   - Ⓒ in the morning
   - Ⓓ at midday

4. Predict how a scorpion is likely to behave towards you if you encounter it. Explain why you think so.

   _____
   _____
   _____

Nonfiction

Fact and Opinion

1

Name _____

When authors write nonfiction, they may include both **facts** and **opinions**. Facts are true. Many sources such as science books or dictionaries will have the same facts.

Opinions tell what a person thinks or feels. Opinions show judgment. People will have different opinions.

Fact: Insects have six legs.   **Opinion: Insects are gross.**

Read the paragraph. Then answer the items.

   A naked mole rat will never win an animal beauty contest. Its wrinkly skin and two large, sharp teeth make it homely. But what it lacks in good looks, it makes up for by being a hard worker. The naked mole rat lives underground. It uses its teeth to dig the tunnels that are its home. These rodents live in colonies of 30 or 40. Like bees, they have a queen whose only job is to have babies—up to 27 at once! Worker mole rats care for the queen and her babies. They also dig the tunnels and collect enough plant roots to feed the colony. Naked mole rats have adapted to living in tunnels. They have lungs like you do. But since there is little air underground, they do not take a breath often. Also, the tunnels are so narrow that they cannot turn around. Luckily they can back up as fast as they can go forward.

1. Write one sentence from the text that is an opinion. Use quotation marks.

   _____

   _____

2. Write two facts to support the idea that naked mole rats are well suited to living underground.

   _____

   _____

3. Does the author have a good opinion of the naked mole rat? Explain your answer.

   _____

   _____

Name _____

Nonfiction
Fact and Opinion

2

When authors write nonfiction, they may include both **facts** and **opinions**.

Research findings, or data, help us know if facts are true. This information is a fact:

  Data show that boys play more team sports in high school than girls do.

Opinions are people's judgments. This is an opinion:

  Soccer takes more skill to play than football.

Read the sentence. Write an **F** on the line if the sentence tells a fact. Write an **O** on the line if the sentence tells an opinion.

1. In 2017, the New England Patriots won Super Bowl 51. _____

2. Super Bowl 51 was the most exciting game of all time. _____

3. Super Bowl 51 was the first superbowl in history to go into overtime. _____

4. Overtime is a 15-minute session in which both teams get three timeouts each. _____

5. The Patriots' quarterback, Tom Brady, is the best football player ever. _____

6. The New England Patriots have won four Super Bowl titles. _____

Answer the items about the sentences above.

7. Explain your answer to sentence number 2.

   _____

   _____

8. Explain your answer to sentence number 6.

   _____

   _____

   _____

Keep Music Education!

Dear School Board Members:

I read that you plan to make big budget cuts to our district's music education programs. I am writing to ask you not to make these cuts. Music education should be part of every child's education. Its benefits extend to other subject areas and life outside of school. Studies show that music helps develop children's language, thinking, and memory skills. That is why children learn the alphabet with a song.

Children who take part in a chorus or band learn teamwork. They have a sense of school pride and a group of friends with the same goals. They are less likely to use drugs or alcohol. Singing or playing an instrument helps to improve a person's listening skills, too.

Children who play musical instruments increase their fine motor skills. This improves their writing, drawing, and keyboarding skills. Learning to play music also helps children believe they can achieve. This "can-do" attitude is helpful in every part of life. In addition, self-confidence helps them to handle anxiety and challenges in all areas of life.

There are more benefits to learning to play an instrument. For example, children learn to set a goal and work toward it. As they practice, they master not just the instrument but reading music as well. Trying to learn a piece of music helps a child to face a reasonable stress and overcome it. And we all know that the ability to handle stress is an important life skill.

Music also teaches math concepts. One of the trickiest things for students of any age to learn is fractions. Musical notes are based on fractions. As a result, students who study music score 23 points higher than average on the math portion and 63 points higher than average on the verbal portion of the SAT.

Visit the website of the National Association for Music Education. It lists even more facts about the benefits of music education. Please do not cut music programs. The day we lose music education will be a sad day for our district.

Sincerely,
Sherinda Lopez, Parent

Name _____

Keep Music Education!

Nonfiction
Fact and Opinion

3

> When authors write nonfiction, they may include both **facts** and **opinions**.
>
> Facts are statements that are true. To identify a fact, ask, *Can this be proven true?*
>
> Opinions show judgment. They cannot be proven true. People may not agree. To identify an opinion, ask, *Can someone disagree?*

Answer the items about the text you read.

1. Which statement from the text reveals the author's opinion?
   - Ⓐ "Children who play musical instruments increase their fine motor skills."
   - Ⓑ "Music also teaches math concepts."
   - Ⓒ "Musical notes are based on fractions."
   - Ⓓ "The day we lose music education will be a sad day for our district."

2. "Music education should be a part of every child's education." Which word makes this statement an opinion?

   _____

   _____

3. "Studies show that music helps develop students' language, thinking, and memory skills." Is this statement a fact or an opinion? Explain how you know.

   _____

   _____

4. Which fact about music education most surprised you?

   _____

   _____

Name _____

Nonfiction
Fact and Opinion

Review

Answer the items.

1. The difference between a fact and an opinion is _____.
   - Ⓐ facts cannot be proven true and opinions can be
   - Ⓑ facts can be proven true and opinions cannot be
   - Ⓒ facts are based on what people think
   - Ⓓ opinions are only based on research and data

2. Write a sentence that tells an opinion.

   _____
   _____

3. Write a sentence that tells a fact.

   _____
   _____

Read the paragraph. Then answer the items.

   Most pearls are made by oysters that live in the world's oceans. The process begins when an irritant, such as a simple piece of sand, enters an oyster's shell. The oyster protects itself by coating the irritant with a shiny mineral. As time passes, more and more layers of this mineral are added to the irritant. Eventually, the irritant becomes a pearl—a natural, shimmering gem that is often worn as jewelry. Pearls are more beautiful than emeralds and rubies. They are the ocean's gift to people who love jewelry.

4. Write one opinion from the text.

   _____
   _____

5. Write one fact from the text.

   _____
   _____

Name _____

Nonfiction

Make Inferences

1

As you read a text, you can **make inferences** to better understand it. When you make an inference, you use what you already know and clues in the text to figure out something that is not directly stated in the text.

Here is an example of an inference:

I read: When the human body is subjected to very hot weather and high temperatures, it sweats. Sweating cools down the body. Some people try to make their bodies produce more sweat in extreme heat. That is probably why spicy food is so popular in places with a hot climate.

I make this inference: Eating spicy food can make you sweat.

Read the paragraph. Then answer the items.

   A cetacean is a marine mammal that lives entirely in water. A marsupial is a mammal as well. Marsupial females have a pouch on their bodies, and they carry their young in it. A primate is a mammal that has hands instead of paws. A rodent is yet another type of mammal. Rodents have front teeth that grow continually. Rodents gnaw on hard materials, such as wood, to wear down their teeth. This is crucial to their survival. A monotreme is a mammal that lays eggs. A platypus is an example of a monotreme.

1. Explain why there are no species of birds or fish discussed in this text.

   _____

   _____

2. Which category of mammals would humans fall under? Explain how you know.

   _____

   _____

3. What happens when a rodent doesn't wear down its teeth?

   _____

   _____

Name _____

Nonfiction

Make Inferences

2

As you read a text, you can **make inferences** to better understand it. When you make an inference, you use what you already know and clues in the text to figure out something that is not directly stated in the text.

Even though you don't read an inference directly, it is a detail that you believe is likely to be true based on the information you do have.

Read the paragraph. Then answer the items.

In 1975, Steve Jobs and Steve Wozniak started Apple, Inc., the amazingly successful computer and media device company. At first, they worked in Jobs' parents' garage. In order to get parts to make their first computer, they sold a van and a calculator.

1. Write one likely reason why Jobs and Wozniak had to work in the garage.

   _____

2. Why did the men have to sell items in order to make a computer?

   _____

Read the paragraph. Then answer the questions.

Have you ever wondered why the letters on a computer keyboard are not in alphabetical order? Christopher Sholes created the arrangement of letters, which is the most common arrangement found on keyboards today, in 1968. It is thought that he did this to make a typewriter that worked better, with keys that wouldn't jam. Previous typewriters had an alphabetical layout. Today, there are other layouts available for keyboards. But most people still prefer the layout that has the letters QWERTY at the top left where the letters begin.

3. What was the problem with typewriters that had an alphabetical layout for the keys?

   it will jam

4. Why is the QWERTY keyboard layout the most popular layout today?

   Its not in alphabetical order and wont jam

Smoke Jumpers: Dropping into Danger

Crackle! Whoosh! Dry grass and dead branches burst into flames. Black smoke hides the sky. A gust of wind carries sparks that turn trees into torches. Soon, a blaze is roaring, and a whole forest is in danger. Can anyone stop this disaster?

Smoke jumpers are firefighters who do the dangerous job of fighting forest fires. They often work in remote areas of thick forest, places where there are no roads or trails, and the only option is to use a parachute to drop right into the fire zone.

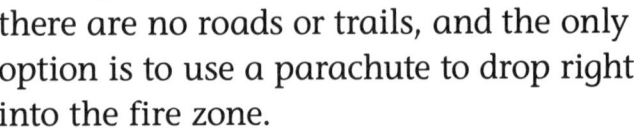

When a fire can be reached only by air, the first step firefighters take is to try to put out the fire with special chemicals. If that does not work, the next step is for helicopters to fly over the fire zone and drop water on the fire. The last choice for firefighters is to send in the smoke jumpers, but they do so only if they must.

When the alarm goes off at the smoke jumpers' base, everyone on duty rushes to get ready. Each smoke jumper puts on a padded jumpsuit and helmet. They grab their parachutes and gear bags. Each bag contains water, gloves, and tools.

Aboard the plane, one smoke jumper acts as a spotter. The spotter uses a map to see where the fire is and determines where the team should land after they jump. It's not easy to pick a landing spot, and the spotter has to be able to make quick decisions.

When the smoke jumpers reach the ground, their first goal is to keep the fire from spreading. They remove brush, logs, leaves, and other dry materials in the fire's path.

The smoke jumpers' second goal is to put out the fire. They mark hot spots with bright yellow tape. The tape shows the air crews where to dump more chemicals and water. The firefighters work fast. Wind is their worst enemy as they try to avoid getting burned or getting smoke in their eyes.

When the blaze is extinguished, the smoke jumpers board helicopters and fly back to base. Without smoke jumpers, a fire can rage on for months, devouring millions of acres of forest.

Name _____

Nonfiction
Make Inferences

3

Smoke Jumpers: Dropping into Danger

> As you read a text, you can **make inferences** to better understand it. When you make an inference, you use what you already know and clues in the text to figure out something that is not directly stated in the text.
>
> Even though you don't read an inference directly, it is a detail that you believe is likely to be true based on the information you do have.

Answer the items about the text you read.

1. Explain why the only option, in some cases, is to jump into the fire zone.

   _____

   _____

2. Why is it the last choice for firefighters to send in the smoke jumpers?

   _____

   _____

   _____

3. How would removing dry materials in the fire's path help keep the fire from spreading?

   _____

   _____

4. Once on the ground, why is the first goal to keep the fire from spreading, rather than to try to put out the fire?

   _____

   _____

5. Why would wind be a smoke jumper's worst enemy in the fire zone?

   _____

   _____

Name _____

Nonfiction
Make Inferences

Review

Answer the items.

1. Explain how to make inferences.

   _____
   _____

2. How is making inferences different from memorizing what the author wrote?

   _____
   _____

Read the paragraph. Then answer the questions.

   Chicken meat has a type of bacteria, called *Salmonella*, that can make people very sick when they eat it. Every year, about one million people are hospitalized with salmonella poisoning. Like most bacteria, salmonella can be killed. It is recommended that people cook chicken until it is 165 degrees Fahrenheit (177 degrees Celsius) or not pink anymore on the inside, so it is safe to eat.

3. How does cooking affect salmonella? Explain how you know.

   _____
   _____
   _____

4. If a person became ill with salmonella poisoning after eating chicken, what inference could you make?

   _____
   _____

5. Do you think research about salmonella poisoning has been done? Explain your answer.

   _____
   _____

Name _____

Nonfiction
Author's Purpose

1

Authors always have a **purpose** for writing a text. These are reasons authors write:

to inform, or tell facts

to entertain, or tell an interesting story

to persuade, or give opinions

to teach, or give instructions about how to do something

Read the paragraph. Then answer the question.

1. Granville T. Woods was an American inventor in the 1800s. When he was ten years old, he went to work in a machine shop. He was very interested in how things worked. In 1884, he got his first patent. A patent is a piece of paper from the government that says that you invented something. Woods got 50 patents in his life.

   What is the author's purpose for writing this paragraph? Explain how you know.

   _____

   _____

2. If you invent something and you don't want other people to copy your idea, you must get a patent from the government. This is how to do it. First, draw pictures or take photos of your invention to show the government. Second, write a description of your invention. Tell what the invention is called and what it does. Next, ask other people to help you get the patent by writing a letter to the government that says the invention is yours.

   What is the author's purpose for writing this paragraph? How do you know?

   _____

   _____

Read the pair of sentences. Then circle the sentence that is meant to persuade.

3. You should read more books about science so you can become a great inventor!

   Every year, thousands of people try to get patents from the U.S. government.

© Evan-Moor Corp. • EMC 2424 • Reading Comprehension Fundamentals   65

Name _____

Nonfiction
Author's Purpose

2

Authors always have a **purpose** for writing a text. To figure out an author's purpose, ask these questions as you read:

  Does the text **inform** me by telling a lot of facts?

  Does the text **entertain** me by telling an interesting story?

  Does the text **persuade** me, or try to get me to have a certain opinion?

  Does the text **teach** me by giving instructions about how to do something?

Hint: If the main purpose is to entertain, the text is probably fiction instead of nonfiction.

Read the paragraph. Then answer the question.

   Some scientists study how well humans remember things. They've discovered that many people can't remember things that happened to them before they were four years old. Also, people remember an event better when they have strong feelings about it. Another thing scientists have discovered is that many people have trouble remembering more than seven numbers in a row.

1. What is the author's purpose for writing this paragraph?
   Ⓐ to persuade
   Ⓑ to entertain
   Ⓒ to inform
   Ⓓ to teach

Answer the items.

2. Which sentence is meant to persuade?
   Ⓐ You should exercise regularly and sleep a lot to improve your memory.
   Ⓑ Scientists have studied the memories of animals.
   Ⓒ Photographs help some people remember experiences they've had.
   Ⓓ Your memory is what helps you remember things that have happened.

3. Explain why you chose the answer you did for number 2.

   _____

   _____

Not-So-Strange Foods

You're on your way home from sports practice. Your stomach grumbles, and you can't wait to eat dinner. All around the world, other people are looking forward to dinner, too. But what they plan to eat may be different from what's on your dinner plate. In some places, people enjoy frog legs, witchetty grubs, earthworm soup, and fried grasshoppers. People eat these foods because they're nutritious. All of these foods have lots of protein, which is something humans need to be healthy and strong.

Large frogs have muscular hind legs, and that is the part that people eat. Their legs can be baked, stewed, grilled, or fried. Many people think that frog legs taste like chicken.

Frog legs

Witchetty grubs are another source of protein. They live underground in the Australian Outback. The Outback is a large area where few people live. It gets very hot, and there's little food and water there. Australians who live there eat the grubs raw or cooked. When raw, the

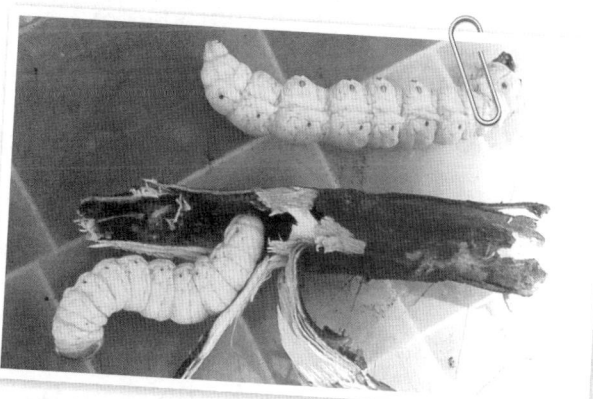

Witchetty grubs

grubs taste like almonds. When roasted, they taste like scrambled eggs. These grubs have saved many people lost in the Outback from starving to death.

In some places, people eat earthworm soup when they have a fever. Earthworms are very nutritious. In addition to protein, they have vitamins and minerals that humans need.

In parts of Mexico, Asia, and Africa, people enjoy eating fried grasshoppers. Some people think they taste like peanuts or shrimp.

Around the world, people eat these foods to stay healthy. And, of course, they like how these foods taste, too!

Grasshoppers

Name _____

Nonfiction
Author's Purpose

3

Not-So-Strange Foods

> Authors always have a **purpose** for writing a text.
> These are reasons authors write:
> - **to inform**, or tell facts
> - **to entertain**, or tell an interesting story
> - **to persuade**, or give opinions
> - **to teach**, or give instructions about how to do something

Answer the items about the text you read.

1. What is the author's purpose for writing this text?
   - Ⓐ to inform you about food sources that you may find unusual
   - Ⓑ to entertain you with stories about foods that you may find unusual
   - Ⓒ to persuade you to eat foods that you may find unusual
   - Ⓓ to teach you how to make foods that you may find unusual

2. Explain how the pictures helped you learn more about these foods.

   _____
   _____
   _____

3. Write two reasons people would want to eat the foods mentioned in the text.

   _____
   _____
   _____

4. In the text, the author compares the foods to other foods you may have tried before. Did this help you learn more about the foods? Tell why or why not.

   _____
   _____
   _____

Name _____

Nonfiction
Author's Purpose

Review

Write the author's purpose next to its description.

1. to tell an interesting story: to _____

2. to tell facts about something: to _____

3. to try to get you to have a certain opinion: to _____

4. to tell you how to do something: to _____

Read the pair of sentences. Then circle the sentence in which the author's purpose is to teach.

5. Homemade cookies are always better than the ones from the store, so it's a good idea to learn how to make your own cookies.

   In a bowl, mix together 1 cup of butter, 1 cup of sugar, 2 cups of flour, and a pinch of salt.

Read the paragraph. Then mark the answer that tells the author's purpose for writing this paragraph.

6. Did you know that people have been eating bread for thousands of years? Bread has been an important food for people around the world for a very long time. Bread is usually made from grains that are ground into a powdery flour or cut into tiny pieces. Many breads are made from wheat, barley, corn, or rye. Bread can be different colors.

   Ⓐ to inform
   Ⓑ to persuade
   Ⓒ to entertain
   Ⓓ to teach

Read the paragraph. Then answer the question.

7. Vegetable snack wraps are the best snack, and more people should eat them. They're so easy to make. And vegetables are healthful, too. If you like salad dressing, cheese, tortillas, and hummus, you'll like vegetable wraps. You can use any vegetables that you like when you make your wraps, so you're sure to enjoy them!

   What is the author's purpose for writing this paragraph? Explain your answer.

   _____

   _____

© Evan-Moor Corp. • EMC 2424 • Reading Comprehension Fundamentals

Name _____

Nonfiction
Text Structure

1

> **Text structure** is the way an author organizes the information in a text. Five common text structures are **description**, **cause and effect**, **compare and contrast**, **sequence**, and **problem and solution**.
>
> You can use these signal words and phrases to help identify the structure of a text:
>
> **description:** for example, such as, for instance, in addition, another
> **cause and effect:** as a result, leads to, because, cause
> **compare and contrast:** both, too, also, instead, rather, similar, different
> **sequence:** first, next, last, then, finally, before, after
> **problem and solution:** prevent, solve, challenge, concern, help

Read the paragraph. Then answer the items.

This is one way to make a poached egg. First, boil a pot of water. Add salt and vinegar to the water. Then, lower the heat, but make sure the water remains hot. Next, break an egg into the hot water. After you put the egg in, quickly cover the pot. Let the egg cook for about 4 or 5 minutes, then lift the egg out of the water with a slotted spoon, or a spoon with holes in it. Finally, put the poached egg on toast or on a plate.

1. This text has a _____ structure.

2. Explain how you know the answer you wrote for number 1.

_____

_____

Read the paragraph. Then answer the items.

It's important to cook eggs well before you eat them. Some people get sick as a result of eating raw eggs. Raw eggs can lead to salmonella poisoning. That's because raw eggs contain salmonella, a kind of bacteria. Cook your eggs to prevent illness.

3. This text has a _____ structure.

4. Explain how you know the answer you wrote for number 3.

_____

_____

Public Transportation Around the World

People around the world rely on public transportation to go from one place to another. There are different kinds of public transportation. In the United States, people ride taxis, ferries, and buses. These are common in other countries, too. But there are many other kinds of public transportation that people use around the world.

Jeepney

In Thailand, for example, you can ride a tuk tuk, which is a three-wheeled motorized vehicle. One person drives the tuk tuk while passengers sit in the back.

Tuk tuk

The cocotaxi is another kind of public transportation in Cuba. This is a motorized vehicle that can carry two or three passengers. It is a small cart-like vehicle that has only three wheels.

In addition to the motorized transportation vehicles mentioned above, the jeepney is yet another popular vehicle that is found in the Philippines. A jeepney is a colorful bus that can carry many people at once.

Cocotaxi

There are also forms of public transportation that are not motorized, such as the cyclo in Vietnam. This is a cycle that has three wheels. The driver sits behind the passengers.

Cyclo

Another form of public transportation that does not have a motor is the hand rickshaw in India. When you ride on one of these rickshaws, a person pulls you as you sit in your seat. This rickshaw has two large wheels.

Rickshaw

If you travel the world, you will see some forms of public transportation are shared by different countries. You will also see some transportation vehicles that are unique to certain places.

Name _____

Nonfiction
Text Structure
2

Public Transportation Around the World

> **Text structure** is the way an author organizes the information in a text. These are five common text structures that authors use:
>
> **Description** texts provide details about a main topic.
>
> **Cause-and-effect** texts explain reasons that things happen.
>
> **Compare-and-contrast** texts explain similarities and differences.
>
> **Sequence** texts explain the order of events or steps in a process.
>
> **Problem-and-solution** texts provide details about a problem, then describe possible solutions to solve or lessen it.

Answer the items about the text you read.

1. The text has a _____ structure.

2. Write three signal words or phrases from the text that support the text structure you wrote for number 1.

   _____   _____   _____

3. Explain how you know the answer you wrote for number 1.

   _____
   _____
   _____

4. Write a sentence that tells the main topic of the text.

   _____
   _____

5. Write two details from the text that tell more about the main topic.

   _____
   _____

Nonfiction
Text Structure

Review

Name _____

Answer the items.

1. Write five common text structures that authors use.

   _____   _____

   _____   _____

   _____

2. Write a description signal word or phrase.   _____

3. Write a cause-and-effect signal word or phrase.   _____

4. Write a compare-and-contrast signal word or phrase.   _____

5. Write a sequence signal word or phrase.   _____

6. Write a problem-and-solution signal word or phrase.   _____

7. Do you think that knowing the text structure can help you to better understand a text? Explain why or why not.

   _____

   _____

   _____

Read the paragraph. Then answer the items.

   Oranges and grapefruits are both citrus fruits that are extremely nutritious. Both oranges and grapefruits have a thick, leathery skin that people usually peel off before eating the fruit. Oranges have a fresh scent, and grapefruits do, too. People squeeze grapefruits and oranges to make juice. Often, grapefruits are more bitter or sour than oranges. Both are usually orange in color, but grapefruits can also be different colors.

8. This text has a _____ structure.

9. Explain how you know the answer you wrote for number 8.

   _____

   _____

Nonfiction
Expository Nonfiction 1

Name _____

Expository nonfiction is text that explains a topic. The purpose of expository nonfiction is to inform by giving facts.

It is common to find expository nonfiction in textbooks, in newspapers, on websites, and in other types of resources.

Read the paragraph. Then answer the items.

In 210 BCE, the first emperor of China was Qin. He had workers build 8,000 warrior figures using terra-cotta, a type of clay. It took the workers 37 years to form all the figures, which are lifesize. The terra-cotta warriors were kept underground. Today, one thousand of them have been uncovered. They were modeled after real warriors, so they are all different sizes, as the real people were. They all have different faces. Some of them are smiling, while others are not. Some are adults, and some are teens. The warrior figures carry real weapons and have clay horses.

1. Explain how you can tell that the author's purpose for writing this paragraph is to inform.

   _____

   _____

2. Write two details about the figures that people have observed.

   _____

   _____

3. By studying these clay figures, what can we learn about the actual warriors in China in the year 210 BCE?

   _____

   _____

The Wreck of the *El Faro*

Ship captains check weather reports and use GPS in order to plan the routes they will take. But no one can control the weather. A storm may increase in strength or suddenly change its direction. When that happens, a ship may be unable to get out of its path. This is what caused a tragedy on October 1, 2015, when *El Faro*, a cargo ship, got caught in a severe storm and wrecked.

On September 29, the 790-foot-long *El Faro* left Jacksonville, Florida, and set sail for Puerto Rico. It carried a cargo of new cars and other merchandise. The experienced captain, Michael Davidson, had evaluated the reports of a tropical storm. But he was certain that the route he chose would keep the ship miles away from the worst weather. He stood on the navigation bridge, which is where the ship is steered from, and gave orders to his crew. Everyone had confidence in Captain Davidson's skill, and the crew members were all experienced.

The next day, while the ship was at sea, the tropical storm turned into Hurricane Joaquin. The hurricane also did something no one had expected: it changed course and headed straight for the ship. Near midnight on September 30, the storm slammed into *El Faro*. It battered the ship with heavy seas and 110-mile-per-hour winds. *El Faro* took on so much water that the cars in its cargo hold began floating. The flooding made the ship lose its engine power. This left it drifting in a sea of giant waves. Those massive waves are almost certainly what destroyed *El Faro*.

Around 7 a.m. on October 1, the captain called in that the ship was in danger. But he and his 32 crew members probably never had a chance to leave the ship. The power of the waves that struck them was tremendous. The waves beat the ship like a giant baseball bat. The waves tore the navigation bridge off the hull. The ship plunged to the sea floor. The hull was found half a mile away from the navigation bridge.

Planes and other ships went to look for survivors. All they found were hundreds of cargo containers sloshing in the waves. Within a month, searchers had located the shipwreck. It lay in deep water 35 miles off Crooked Island in the Bahamas. It took months of searching to find its voyage data recorder. This is something that all ships have, that records every sound that happens on the navigation bridge. The recording ends abruptly at 7:39 a.m.

This photo shows another ship that wrecked and sank. This is not *El Faro*.

Name _____

Nonfiction
Expository Nonfiction

2

The Wreck of the *El Faro*

> **Expository nonfiction** is text that explains a topic.
> The purpose of expository nonfiction is to inform by giving facts.
>
> Visual information can provide additional information in an expository text. Expository nonfiction may include dates, times, definitions, descriptive details, and other types of information.

Answer the items about the text you read.

1. Explain how you can tell that the author's purpose for writing this text is to inform.

   _____

   _____

2. How did the dates and times help you better understand the topic?

   _____

   _____

3. Captain Davidson and his crew weren't worried about the tropical storm at first? Why?

   _____

   _____

4. What descriptive details helped you better understand the topic?

   _____

   _____

   _____

5. How did the picture help you to better understand what happened to *El Faro*?

   _____

76 Reading Comprehension Fundamentals • EMC 2424 • © Evan-Moor Corp.

Name _____

Nonfiction
Expository Nonfiction

Review

Answer the items.

1. Explain the author's purpose for writing an expository nonfiction text.

   _____
   _____

2. Write two types of resources where can you find expository nonfiction text.

   _____
   _____

3. Write three types of facts or details that an expository nonfiction text can include.

   _____
   _____

4. How can visual information provide additional support in an expository nonfiction text?

   _____
   _____

5. Write one reason why you would choose to read an expository nonfiction text.

   _____
   _____

Read the paragraph. Then answer the item.

6. The huge, hairy bat flew around our living room wildly. I screamed, and Dad swatted at it with a newspaper. Mom grabbed a broom and tried to steer the bat out the window. We had no idea how it got into our house, but we definitely wanted it out.

    Is this an example of expository nonfiction? Explain why or why not.

    _____
    _____

© Evan-Moor Corp. • EMC 2424 • Reading Comprehension Fundamentals

Name _____

Nonfiction
Persuasive Nonfiction

1

> In a **persuasive nonfiction** text, the author tries to convince the reader to believe something or to do something. The author usually gives reasons to try to persuade the reader.
>
> Advertisements are always persuasive text. They use a headline or short statements to get the reader's attention.

Read the email. Then answer the items.

Subject: Sale for our VIP Customers!

From: Skateboards Unlimited

It's time to buy! All skateboards slashed to clearance prices!
As a VIP customer at Skateboards Unlimited, you get first pick of our best inventory. Go to www.skateboardsunlimited.com and enter the code: VIPcustomer5894. These are the best prices of the season! Hurry and buy a skateboard today! Quantities are limited!

---

1. The email says that "quantities are limited" because the people who wrote it _____.

   Ⓐ want customers to think that they will run out of skateboards soon
   Ⓑ want customers to think that there aren't any good skateboards left
   Ⓒ want customers to think that they will get a bigger discount
   Ⓓ want customers to think that they have a lot of time to buy

2. Write phrases or sentences from the email that try to persuade the customer to buy.

   _____

   _____

3. Why do you think so many exclamation points are used in the email?

   _____

   _____

4. If you were a VIP customer, would you buy a skateboard? Explain why or why not.

   _____

Experience Alaska!

Where can you go to see the ghostly northern lights, ancient glaciers, and North America's tallest mountain? If you said Alaska, you'd be right. Alaska is one of the best tourist destinations in the United States. There is so much to see and do that most vacationers spend two weeks. Visiting Alaska is an amazing, magical experience, especially for those who enjoy nature.

Why do visitors flock to this huge, far-north state? It is one of the world's last remaining wilderness areas. It has fewer people per square mile than any other part of the United States. It has more miles of sea coast than all the other sea coasts in the United States put together. It features crystal clear lakes, vast pine forests, gurgling rivers, and lots of wildlife. Alaska is the only place left in the country to get a frontier experience.

Alaska has millions of acres of park land. Driving through Denali National Park lets you view wildlife in a natural setting. Wolves, grizzly bears, moose, and caribou live among the snow-capped peaks, plains, and glacier-fed rivers. The park also has a set of well-preserved fossilized dinosaur footprints. If you're a climber, you can scale Denali, the highest peak on the continent.

Take a flight in a small airplane while your pilot points out grizzly bears fishing for salmon in roaring rivers. Soar over miles of forests and glimpse smoking volcanoes in the distance. It will be the best plane ride you ever take!

Go on a boat ride through Glacier Bay National Park. Majestic mountains surround sparkling, clear lakes. The 4,000-year-old glaciers slowly slide down the mountain slopes. When they reach the water's edge, the glaciers calve, dropping a huge ice chunk into the water. The ice crashes into the lake and floats as an iceberg. It slowly melts. The Johns Hopkins Glacier calves large pieces of ice. Boats must stay 2 miles away from its edge. If you are lucky enough to see a glacier calve, it is a once-in-a-lifetime experience.

Come see Alaska. You won't be disappointed!

Name _____

Nonfiction
Persuasive Nonfiction

2

Experience Alaska!

In a **persuasive nonfiction** text, the author tries to convince the reader to believe something or to do something. The author uses language that shows opinions or judgment.

   The author may use positive words such as *best*, *amazing*, and *special*.

   The author may use negative words such as *worst*, *boring*, or *hideous*.

Persuasive text is in advertisements, catalogs, travel brochures, and on websites.

Answer the items about the text you read.

1. Which of these statements from the text is an opinion?
   Ⓐ "Come see Alaska."
   Ⓑ "The park also has a set of well-preserved fossilized dinosaur footprints."
   Ⓒ "It has fewer people per square mile than any other part of the United States."
   Ⓓ "Alaska is one of the best tourist destinations in the United States."

2. What is the author trying to persuade you to do or believe? Explain your answer.

   _____

   _____

3. Write a statement from the text that uses persuasive words.

   _____

   _____

4. Where would you most likely read this text?

   _____

   _____

5. Did the author persuade you to visit Alaska? Explain your response to the text.

   _____

   _____

Name _____

Nonfiction

Persuasive Nonfiction

Review

Answer the item.

1. An author writes a persuasive nonfiction text to _____.
   - Ⓐ get the reader to keep reading
   - Ⓑ tell about an item or a place
   - Ⓒ convince the reader to believe something or do something
   - Ⓓ convince the reader that the author knows everything

Circle the pair of sentences if it is an example of persuasive nonfiction.

2. Don't eat at Ralph's Burgers! The French fries are disgusting!

3. Seashells by the Shore opened for business in 2014. Since then, they have hired six employees.

4. The best way to travel to Monterey is on the most scenic highway in the world, the Pacific Coast Highway.

Read the paragraph. Then explain what makes this a persuasive nonfiction text.

5.   If you are one of the few people who have not heard of the best sport in the world, I'd love to tell you all about it! You will never have more fun than when you play pickleball! Pickleball is a paddle sport that combines tennis, badminton, and ping pong! It is played both indoors and outdoors on a badminton-sized court that has a net similar to a tennis net. Pickleball is played with a paddle and a plastic ball with holes. Now doesn't that sound awesome? If your answer to that question is "yes," you are in good company. According to the Sports and Fitness Industry Association's 2016 Participant Report, there are more than 2.5 million people playing pickleball in the United States! After all, who wants to play a boring game of tennis when you can play pickleball! Find a pickleball court in your area and join the fun today!

_____

_____

_____

_____

Name _____

Nonfiction

Narrative Nonfiction

1

> **Narrative nonfiction** tells a story about true events experienced by real people. Although narrative nonfiction has literary elements, it is based on facts. The story's settings, characters, and events are true.
>
> When people write a story about their own lives, the text is called a **memoir**. A memoir is a kind of narrative nonfiction.

Read the memoir. Then answer the items.

   When I was six years old, my mom asked me to call Grandpa and invite him over for dinner one night. I called and asked Grandpa if he'd like to come over. Grandpa said, "Well, now, that depends on what you're having." I asked Mom what she was preparing. I reported that the meal was old, rotten potatoes.
   Grandpa said, "Really? Old, rotten potatoes?"
   I said, "Don't you like them?" I was disappointed, thinking that he wouldn't come over for dinner.
   Grandpa chuckled and said, "No one I know likes to eat old, rotten potatoes. But I'm pretty sure your mom is making au gratin potatoes. I'll see you in half an hour."

1. Explain what is causing the confusion in the story.

   _____

   _____

   _____

2. From the way the story is told, do you think that the narrator now understands what caused the confusion in the story? Explain your answer.

   _____

   _____

   _____

3. Can narrative nonfiction contain humor, or funny parts? Explain your answer.

   _____

   _____

An African Adventure

Christina Dodwell and Lesley Jamieson were young women when they decided to do something adventurous. In 1975, the two set out on a year-long trip across Africa. They wanted to see as much of the continent as possible. They started their trip with two other people. Everything went smoothly until the night after they crossed the Sahara Desert.

Sahara Desert

When the women awoke the next morning, they found that their fellow travelers had stolen their car and abandoned them! Christina and Lesley were all alone in Nigeria. They had no food or map and few supplies. But they were determined to see more of Africa, so they set off on foot.

They trekked for miles over dry, rugged land. They walked from village to village, getting rides from friendly people when possible. Eventually they found two semi-wild horses. The women knew they would be able to cover more miles on horseback than on foot. They tamed the horses and rode them.

They rode for weeks. All along the way, they met new friends. Everywhere they went, people invited them into their homes. They danced with people, helped cook traditional African meals, and played games with children. If Christina and Lesley couldn't find a village by the end of a day's ride, they ate wild plants and insects instead of traditional food. At all times they kept a close watch for deadly snakes and scorpions.

In a small city, they bought a loaf of bread, a jar of jam, and a dugout canoe. (This kind of canoe is a log with the material cut from the middle of it.) They paddled the canoe a thousand miles down the Congo River. It was exhausting. Their arms felt like noodles from so much paddling. Yet they had to stay alert. In that river, crocodiles and hippos have been known to flip canoes.

After about a year of traveling, Lesley had experienced enough adventure. She left Africa. Christina continued traveling around the continent for two more years. During that time, she covered 20,000 miles alone.

These daring women showed the world that they weren't afraid to explore and take risks. They made many friends along the way, and their story still inspires adventurous travelers today.

Name _____

An African Adventure

Nonfiction
Narrative Nonfiction
2

> **Narrative nonfiction** tells a story about true events experienced by real people. Narrative nonfiction reads like a story, unlike many other types of nonfiction, which read like an essay or a news article.

Answer the items about the text you read.

1. Explain why Lesley and Christina's story may inspire other people.

   _____
   _____
   _____

2. Write two things that Lesley and Christina did that could be considered adventurous.

   _____
   _____

3. Why do you think the author claims that Lesley and Christina took "risks"? Write three things the women did that could be considered "risky."

   _____
   _____
   _____

4. Do you think that most people would do the things that Lesley and Christina did? Explain why or why not.

   _____
   _____

5. What is your favorite part of Lesley and Christina's story? Explain why.

   _____
   _____

Name _____

Nonfiction

Narrative Nonfiction

Review

Answer the items.

1. In your own words, explain what narrative nonfiction is.

   _____

2. Explain how narrative nonfiction can be similar to a fictional story.

   _____

   _____

3. Explain how narrative nonfiction is different from other kinds of nonfiction texts.

   _____

   _____

4. Do you think that a narrative nonfiction story can be just as interesting as a fiction story? Explain why or why not.

   _____

   _____

Read the paragraph. Then answer the question.

5.   Many centuries ago, the kings and queens of Great Britain hired jesters, who were basically comedians. The jester's job was to make everyone in the palace laugh. During the twelfth century, King Henry I had a jester named Rayer. Rayer used to make the king laugh by making jokes about other people whom the king knew. Although Rayer often acted silly, he was actually a rather intelligent and serious man. After working as a jester for some time, Rayer founded St. Bartholomew's Hospital, in London, in the year 1123. The hospital still stands as the oldest hospital in England.

St. Bart's Hospital in London

What additional details could have been included in this narrative nonfiction text?

_____

_____

© Evan-Moor Corp. • EMC 2424 • Reading Comprehension Fundamentals

Name _____

Nonfiction
Descriptive Nonfiction

1

> **Descriptive nonfiction** provides details about a main topic. The topic can be a person, place, thing, or event. Descriptive nonfiction provides sensory details, or details about how the main topic **looks**, **feels**, **tastes**, **smells**, or **sounds**.

Read the paragraph. Then answer the items.

  The Virginia Beach Boardwalk is one of the best walkways in the U.S. Pedestrians and bicyclists enjoy the three-mile-long cement path. It is as wide as a city street and lined with tall hotels. The aromas of many different kinds of food mingle in the air. Hot dog grills sizzle. Candy and donut shops display colorful sweets in their shop windows. Nice restaurants appear well lit and welcoming. At each block, there is a ramp down to the soft, sandy beach, which is met by the sparkling Atlantic Ocean's waves. On a sunny day, the gentle, salty, fishy breeze and the cawing of gulls flying overhead gives you the sense of being in paradise.

1. Write words or phrases from the paragraph that describe the Virginia Beach Boardwalk.

    how it looks: _____

    how it smells: _____

    how it feels: _____

    how it tastes: _____

    how it sounds: _____

2. Did the details in the text help you picture the Virginia Beach Boardwalk in your mind? Explain your answer.

    _____

3. Would you want to spend time at the Virginia Beach Boardwalk? Explain why or why not.

    _____

    _____

The Farmers' Market

Every weekend, many people go to the farmers' market. There is so much to buy, eat, and see that it's an exciting place to be.

Early in the morning, the farmers and other vendors arrive, usually in pickup trucks or vans. They set up tables, place their goods on them, and post price signs. Many set up colorful striped awnings to shade their goods from the weather. The vendors work fast, knowing that as soon as the gates open, a flood of people will enter.

A lot of booths sell food. Some farmers sell freshly picked vegetables like potatoes, sweet corn, green beans, and eggplants. They sell strawberries, peaches, blueberries, and other luscious fruits. Beekeepers offer jars of honey taken from their own beehives.

A crowd often forms around the booths where people sell homemade breads, muffins, pies, and cakes. The people are drawn by the delicious odors of the baked goods. They especially like it if the bakers offer samples!

Some vendors don't sell food. They sell crafts such as colorful quilts, scented candles, and handmade soaps. In spring, growers come to the farmers' market. They offer small flowering plants in trays. Buyers take them home to plant in their own gardens. Growers also sell flowering plants in large hanging baskets, planters, and urns. Gardeners

barter with the growers. They try to get the best price for yellow daisies, red begonias, and dark pink geraniums. Occasionally, the growers will have small shrubs and rose bushes to sell as well.

The farmers' market is a great place to eat. You can get caramel popcorn, gooey donuts, slices of pizza with different toppings, and tacos with spicy salsa. Wash it all down with chilled lemonade or iced tea. Yum!

There are things just for kids, too. They can get their faces painted with bright colors and designs. Sometimes clowns twist balloons into animal shapes. Jugglers walk among the crowd tossing flaming sticks into the air. Spending a day at the farmers' market is always fun!

Name _____

Nonfiction
Descriptive Nonfiction

2

The Farmers' Market

> **Descriptive nonfiction** provides details about a main topic. The topic can be a person, place, thing, or event. Descriptive nonfiction provides sensory details, or details about how the main topic **looks, feels, tastes, smells, or sounds**.

Answer the items about the text you read.

1. Explain how the details in the text helped you picture the farmers' market in your mind.

   _____
   _____
   _____

2. In your own words, describe the smells at the farmers' market.

   _____
   _____
   _____

3. What are three colors would you likely see at the farmers' market? Explain how you know.

   _____
   _____

4. What details in the text suggest that the farmers' market would be entertaining?

   _____
   _____

5. Which part of the farmers' market would you enjoy most? Explain why.

   _____
   _____

Reading Comprehension Fundamentals • EMC 2424 • © Evan-Moor Corp.

Nonfiction
Descriptive Nonfiction
Review

Name _____

Answer the items.

1. In your own words, explain what a descriptive nonfiction text is.

   _____

   _____

2. Explain what sensory details are.

   _____

   _____

   _____

3. How good would a descriptive nonfiction text be without sensory details? Explain your answer.

   _____

   _____

   _____

Read the paragraph. Then answer the question.

4. The aye-aye is a primate that looks so unusual, the people who first saw it thought that it was a rodent. The aye-aye lives in Madagascar, an island nation near Africa. It has large yellow eyes that are round, and dark rounded ears that stick up above its head. The aye-aye is covered in thick black or gray fur. It has a small mouth and large front teeth. Its face is usually white, which makes its large eyes stand out even more. The aye-aye is quite small, weighing only about 5 pounds and being about 16 inches in length.

Does the text do a good job of describing the aye-aye, according to the picture? Explain your opinion.

_____

_____

_____

Name _____

Fiction

Character

1

When you think about a **character**, it helps you to better understand a story. You can learn a lot about a character by paying attention to details in the story. Look at these details in the story:

- what a character says
- how a character does things
- what a character enjoys

Read the paragraph. Then circle the best description of the character.

1. Rebecca and her family went hiking. Rebecca stepped quietly along the trail, her ears listening for each and every sound. She smiled as the songs of chickadees and doves drifted through the air. While her brother rushed up the trail, Rebecca went slowly, carefully observing everything around her. She stooped down, moved some dried leaves aside, and found a newt. She watched it wriggle under a log, said goodbye to it, and hurried to catch up with her family.

    Rebecca is impatient.   Rebecca loves nature.   Rebecca likes newts.

2. Taylor was on a hike with his family. He rushed ahead of them, running along the winding trail, leaping over boulders, and ducking under branches. He found a fallen branch and pretended it was a hockey stick. Whack! He sent an acorn sailing into the air. "He shoots, he scores!" Taylor yelled. Next, he saw a curved branch up high. It looked like a basketball hoop. He tossed a pinecone up through it. "Yes!" he shouted.

    Taylor likes hiking.   Taylor loves sports.   Taylor likes pinecones.

Answer the item.

3. Think about the characters in the paragraphs above. Do you think that they would enjoy hiking together? Explain why you think so.

_____

_____

_____

Name _____

Fiction

Character

2

> When you think about a **character**, it helps you to better understand the story. A character can make events happen in the story.
> Ask these questions when you read:
>
> Does a character have a strong opinion?
>
> Does a character feel a certain way?
>
> What is important to the character?

Read the paragraph. Then answer the question.

1. Bao was in Mr. Gibb's after-school program. Today, Mr. Gibb was showing the students how to make cookies. Bao, Izzie, and Leana were in a group. Izzie did not like cooking and wanted to be done quickly. Leana reminded her that they needed to measure out ingredients correctly, but Izzie didn't care. Leana sighed when their cookies came out of the oven. They were too hard and had no flavor.

   Which character had the biggest influence on the final result? Explain your answer.

   _____

   _____

Read the paragraph. Then answer the items.

   For An-Kor's tenth birthday, his parents said that they would throw him a party and invite all his relatives. But An-Kor didn't want a party this year. He just wanted to go to the movies with his friends. An-Kor's parents told him that his grandparents would be sad if he didn't have a party for his tenth birthday. Even though he didn't feel like it, An-Kor agreed to have a party so his grandparents would be happy.

2. Write one thing that is important to An-Kor. Explain why you think so.

   _____

   _____

   _____

3. Circle the words that describe An-Kor.

   selfish   thoughtful   stubborn   understanding   rude

Danger on the Mountain

Lhamo trudged slowly up the steep slope of the mountain. She and her climbing team formed a long line. They climbed steadily upward. After each step, Lhamo rested for a moment to catch her breath.

After weeks on the mountain, the team decided that today would be the day that they would reach the summit, or the top of the mountain. The team left camp in the middle of the night with the hope of reaching the summit by midmorning. On the mountain top, they would take pictures and rest for a bit. Then they would head back down to camp before the midday storm that arrived every day. All climbers tried to avoid the storms because it's dangerous to be near the summit when strong winds and snow are blowing around.

At the head of the line was Jack. He really wanted to reach the summit on this day, even if there was danger along the way. Lhamo could see that Jack was moving much too fast. He wasn't waiting for his teammates. He hurried ahead and grabbed a rope hanging from above. It was a rope that climbers used to go up and down that section. Another team was just about to come down the rope, but now they had to wait while Jack climbed up.

Lhamo was annoyed. Jack knew that there were safety rules that all climbers followed on the mountain. One of the rules was to always let climbers come down first. By ignoring the rules, Jack was putting other climbers in danger.

Lhamo checked her watch. Her team didn't have much time before they'd have to turn back down, whether they'd reached the summit or not.

The team waited while the other climbing team came down. A few minutes later, Lhamo had climbed the rope. She could see the mountain's summit. The team was so close! Lhamo couldn't wait to see the view from the top. But then she heard a groan. Jack was lying in the snow!

Lhamo told the rest of her team to continue climbing. She took one last look at the summit. Then she stooped over Jack. "I have to get you back down the mountain for your safety!" she said. Slowly, she led Jack back down. Neither of them got to the summit that day.

Name _____

Fiction
Character

3

Danger on the Mountain

Character traits describe characters. These are examples of character traits:

| kind | hopeful | selfish | patient |
| thoughtful | calm | fair | trustworthy |

Answer the items about the story you read.

1. Which character traits describe Lhamo?
   - Ⓐ weak and angry
   - Ⓑ sad and confused
   - Ⓒ helpful and responsible
   - Ⓓ selfish and impatient

2. Explain why you chose the answer you did for number 1.

   _____

   _____

3. Which character traits describe Jack?
   - Ⓐ careless and selfish
   - Ⓑ quiet and shy
   - Ⓒ helpful and responsible
   - Ⓓ slow and careful

4. Explain why you chose the answer you did for number 3.

   _____

   _____

5. Explain how the story could've been different if Jack had traits similar to Lhamo's.

   _____

   _____

Name _____

Fiction

Character

Review

Answer the items.

1. Which one can be a character trait?
   - Ⓐ the five senses
   - Ⓑ the plot
   - Ⓒ a character
   - Ⓓ serious

2. Explain how a character's actions can change how the story ends.

   _____
   _____
   _____

3. Explain why a character's opinions or feelings are important in a story.

   _____
   _____

4. Explain how a character's choices can affect the other characters in the story.

   _____
   _____
   _____

5. Write four character traits that you can think of.

   _____   _____

   _____   _____

Read the paragraph. Then write a character trait to complete the sentence.

6. Luigi has three cookies. His little sister doesn't have any cookies. She cries because she wants one, and she sees Luigi eating one. Luigi quickly eats all of the cookies before his mom tells him that he must share.

   Luigi is a _____ person.

Name _____

Fiction
Setting

1

The **setting** is the time and place of a story. The setting can be a natural environment or a man-made place. When you read, look for words and phrases that describe the following things:

  how the setting looks

  how the character feels in the setting

  if the story happens in the past, present, or future

Read the paragraph. Then answer the items.

  Ikiaq marched through the deep snow, dragging the heavy sled behind him. An icy wind whipped through his thick coat, making him shiver. The dark shapes of spruce trees stood out against the dull gray sky. Ikiaq saw a bit of orange far away, where the sun was setting. He reached the pile of firewood, brushed off some snow that was on it, and loaded wood into the sled. On his return trip to the house, he kept his eyes on the family room window. Icicles hung around the window, but a cozy light glowed inside. Soon he'd be by the warm fire inside with his family.

1. Explain where Ikiaq is and what he's doing.

   _____

   _____

2. Explain why Ikiaq's family needs firewood.

   _____

   _____

3. If the setting were different, would Ikiaq's actions be different in the story? Explain your answer.

   _____

   _____

4. Describe how you would you feel if you were in this setting.

   _____

© Evan-Moor Corp. • EMC 2424 • Reading Comprehension Fundamentals

Fiction

Setting

2

The **setting** is the time and place that a story happens. Ask yourself these questions when you read:

Are there objects in the story that are from a long time ago?

Does the story include objects that people use today?

Is the story in the past, present, or future?

Does the setting make a character feel happy or unhappy?

Read the paragraph. Then answer the items.

Jodi and Tyson waited in the car at the gas station while their mom went inside to pay for fuel. "The smell of the air here is making me sick," moaned Jodi. Tyson had also noticed that the air smelled strongly of gas. He looked around for his mom. He could see her standing in line, waiting to pay. His mom had let him play games on her phone during the car ride. Tyson gave the phone to Jodi so she could play games and feel better. When mom got in the car, she could see that Jodi wasn't feeling well. Jodi and Tyson's mom quickly drove away from the gas station.

1. Mark the details that describe the setting.
   Ⓐ in car, park, sunny
   Ⓑ in car, gas station, strong smell
   Ⓒ in car, driving, raining
   Ⓓ in car, playing games, driving

2. Do you think this story happens in the past, present, or future? Explain why you think so.

   _____

   _____

3. How does the setting affect Jodi and Tyson?

   _____

   _____

The Clever Rabbit

Long ago, in a place where trees and animals could speak with humans, a man wandered along a mountain path. He heard a groan. He peered into a deep pit and spotted a fierce-looking tiger.

"Help!" the tiger begged. "I'm trapped, and I can't get out!"

The man wanted to help, but the beast's sharp fangs made him nervous. The tiger guessed what the man was thinking, and said, "You have no need to fear me. I promise, I won't eat you."

Even though the man didn't feel certain, he believed the tiger because the tiger made a promise. So the man snapped a long branch off a pine tree and lowered it for the tiger to grab. After pulling the tiger out, the man laid back and closed his eyes. But instantly he opened his eyes again, fearfully. The tiger was stepping quickly toward him.

"I'm hungry," the tiger growled.

Jumping to his feet, the man cried, "You made a promise!"

The tiger snickered. "Yes, but now that I'm free, I can do whatever I please."

"That's not fair!" the man cried, anxiously looking around. "What do you think, Pine Tree?" the man asked.

The pine tree leaned forward and said, "You snapped off my branch without asking me first, so I believe it's quite fair for the tiger to eat you." The tiger moved closer to the man.

"Wait!" the man cried. "I see an ox grazing in that meadow. Let's see what she thinks of this situation."

As the ox listened to both sides of the story, she kept looking at the man's shoes. Then she angrily said, "Your shoes were made from an ox's hide. I see no reason why the tiger shouldn't eat you."

The tiger showed his sharp teeth. Just then, a rabbit hopped out from the trees.

"Let's see what that rabbit thinks!" the man begged. The tiger grumbled as he grew hungrier.

The rabbit listened to the man's story. Then the rabbit said, "Just so I understand everything correctly, Tiger, can you show me exactly how and where you were trapped?"

The tiger climbed down into the pit. "Like this, see?" he roared.

"Excellent," the rabbit said. "In my opinion, the problem began when this man helped you. So, it'd be best if we leave everything how it was before."

The clever rabbit hopped away, the man continued on his journey, and the tiger groaned at the bottom of the pit.

Name _____

Fiction
Setting

3

The Clever Rabbit

The **setting** is the time and place of a story. When you think about the setting, you can better understand the story. Think about the following things when you read:

The setting can cause characters to do certain things in the story.

The setting can be realistic, or like a place in the real world. Or the setting can be make-believe or magical, unlike a place in the real world.

The setting can make events or other elements in the story possible or impossible.

Answer the items about the story you read.

1. Is the setting realistic or make-believe? Explain why you think so.

   _____

   _____

2. In the story, the man uses things in his environment. Explain how the ox and the pine tree feel about the man doing this.

   _____

   _____

3. Explain why the pit is an important part of the story.

   _____

   _____

   _____

4. Write two things that would be different in the story if there were no pit in the setting.

   _____

   _____

   _____

Name _____

Fiction
Setting

Review

Answer the items.

1. Explain what the setting in a story is.

   _____

   _____

2. Explain how the setting can cause characters to feel a certain way.

   _____

   _____

3. Write one question you can ask yourself about the setting of a story.

   _____

   _____

Read the paragraph. Then answer the items.

   Tiana's family is at a wedding in a hotel ballroom. The huge ballroom looks pretty, with fancy lights and tablecloths, but it's freezing inside. Tiana wore a new dress, and she wanted to show it to her aunts, who would be at the wedding, too. But Tiana had to borrow a big sweater that her dad had in the car because she felt so cold. It was so big that it pretty much covered her whole dress! Tiana sat at a table near some sound speakers. Suddenly, loud music started playing from them. It was so loud that she couldn't hear anything else. A little while later, Tiana smelled a strong odor. It was the dinner being served. She didn't think it smelled very tasty at all. Tiana wasn't having very much fun at this wedding.

4. Explain how the setting affects Tiana's decision to show her dress to her aunts.

   _____

   _____

5. Is the setting realistic or make-believe? Explain how you know.

   _____

   _____

Name _____

Fiction

Plot

1

> When you think about a story's **plot**, you think about how the events in the story are arranged. The author arranges the sequence of events in a certain way to make the story interesting. The events in the plot are related to each other.
>
> As you read a story, think about why certain events happen before others.
>
> Think about how the problems in the story make the story interesting.

Read the sentences. Explain whether or not the sequence of events and details makes sense. Then explain why you think so.

1. Now Rita is able to work on the school computer.

   Rita is trying to log in to the school computer to do research, but it isn't working.

   Rita decides to use the school computer to do research.

   Rita's teacher helps her log in to the school computer.

   Rita has been assigned to write a research report about camels.

   _____
   _____
   _____

Read the pair of story ideas. Circle the story idea that you think is the most interesting. Then explain why you think so.

2. Shankar's report slipped out of his hand. The wind blew it across the street, and it landed in a puddle. Then a child stepped on it. Shankar didn't have another copy, so he had to pull it out of the puddle and turn it in to his teacher, wet and with a footprint on it.

   Shankar printed out his report. On the way to school, he kept it safe in his backpack. In the classroom, he stapled the pages together and turned it in to his teacher.

   _____
   _____

Name _____

Fiction

Plot

2

> When you think about a story's **plot**, you think about the pattern of events in the story and how the events relate to each other. The author arranges the events in a certain way to make the story interesting. This is a common plot pattern:
>
> In the beginning, things are good, but then a problem is introduced.
>
> In the middle, the problem becomes more complicated or gets worse as the characters try to deal with it.
>
> The most exciting part of the story is when a character must act to solve the problem.
>
> In the end, there is a solution to the problem in the story.

Read the paragraph. Then answer the question.

1. Everybody knew that Greg was dreadfully afraid of spiders. Whenever his family members heard him scream, they ran to his aid. But one night, Greg was home alone when he saw the biggest, hairiest spider he had ever seen, running across the sofa. "Ahh!" he screamed, as he realized nobody was there to help him. Greg sprang up from his seat and ran to the kitchen. He grabbed a bottle of spray cleaner and tried to spray the spider, but the little creature darted underneath a sofa cushion. This made Greg even more terrified. He rolled up a magazine, lifted the cushion, and started swatting. The spider jumped onto the floor. "Ahh!" Greg screamed again. Then he ran to the closet, grabbed a broom, and started pushing the spider toward the front door. He opened the door, pushed the spider out, and quickly shut the door. Breathing heavily, he suddenly felt brave and proud. "I got rid of the spider myself, and I didn't even hurt the spider," he thought happily. After that night, Greg still screamed when he saw spiders, but he didn't need anyone else to help him.

   Does this story have a common plot pattern? Explain why you think so.

   _____
   _____
   _____
   _____
   _____

© Evan-Moor Corp. • EMC 2424 • Reading Comprehension Fundamentals

Irwin and Sir Grunk

The village of Kree was a peaceful place. Most folks spent their time tending their gardens and visiting friends. There was just one problem in Kree, and its name was Sir Grunk. Sir Grunk was the meanest, rudest citizen in the village. He bullied his neighbors, picking plants out of their gardens and yelling at them.

Irwin, a citizen of Kree, had finally had enough. "Someone should do something about Sir Grunk," he said.

"Not I," Gillen said.

"Nor I," Renway said.

Everyone in Kree, including Irwin, said "Not I" to standing up to Sir Grunk. So, Irwin decided to go on a quest to find a hero for Kree. "If everyone in Kree is too afraid of Sir Grunk, I may find a hero somewhere else," he thought.

Irwin walked very far. He crossed through fields and forests. Eventually, he came to a river with a fallen tree going over it, so he decided to cross.

The tree was very narrow, though, and Irwin fell down into the fast-moving water. After the river's current took him far away, he finally grabbed ahold of a weed on the riverbank and pulled himself out. "Ugh, I'm absolutely soaked!" Irwin said, shivering.

Before Irwin could dry off, he noticed a cave up the road. He heard a low rumbling, and billows of smoke floated out. Irwin wondered who (or what) was there, when a fierce-looking ogre poked its head out. The ogre saw Irwin.

"Lunch time!" the ogre said, licking its lips. It reached into its pocket and took out a fireball. The ogre threw the fireball at Irwin. As soon as it hit him, though, it sizzled and disappeared. "You put out my fireball!" the ogre moaned.

"Serves you right!" Irwin said. "That's because I'm all soaked from the river." The ogre disappeared back into its cave, and Irwin thought about continuing his quest. Then a brilliant idea popped into his head. "Hey, I defeated an ogre!" he exclaimed. "Maybe I'm the hero that Kree needs."

Irwin decided to head back to Kree. He went back the way he came, over the river, through the forests and fields.

Back in Kree, Irwin stomped straight over to Sir Grunk's house. Irwin banged on the door so loudly that the whole village heard and stood behind him.

"Sir Grunk," he said, "you will stop bullying others and stop being cruel. And if you don't stop, I'll make you leave Kree." Everyone gasped.

Seeing Irwyn's courage made the other villagers feel brave. They didn't let Sir Grunk bully them anymore, and he eventually left Kree for good.

Name _____

Fiction
Plot

3

Irwin and Sir Grunk

> In a story, the **plot** is the sequence of events and how the events relate to each other. The way the events are arranged makes the story more interesting. Think about the following questions when you think about plot:
>
> What problem is introduced in the beginning of the story?
>
> How does the character try to solve the problem in the middle of the story?
>
> How do things get more difficult for the main character in the story?
>
> How does the problem get solved at the end of the story?

Answer the items about the story you read.

1. Describe the problem at the beginning of the story.

   _____

   _____

2. Did Irwin have a hard time in the middle of the story? Use details from the story to explain why you think so.

   _____

   _____

3. What was the most exciting part of the story? Explain why you think so.

   _____

   _____

4. What made Irwin think that he could be a hero?

   _____

   _____

5. Would the story have been as interesting without the problems? Explain your answer.

   _____

   _____

Name _____

Fiction

Plot

Review

Answer the items.

1. Explain in your own words what the plot of a story is.

   _____

   _____

2. Explain why problems are an important part of a story's plot.

   _____

   _____

3. Why is it important to look closely at the beginning, middle, and end when you think about the plot of a story?

   _____

   _____

Match the part of the story with the plot pattern description.

4. beginning •   • The problem is solved.

   middle •   • The problem is introduced.

   end •   • The character deals with the problem.

Read the paragraph. Then write **beginning**, **middle**, or **end** to tell which part of the plot is missing.

5.   Denny loves trying new hobbies, and he has done a lot of them over the years. In the past, he had been in singing club, chess club, sports club, and drawing club. He also played soccer one year, and another year he played basketball. Last year, he did horseback riding. This year, though, Denny has so many after-school hobbies that he doesn't have time to take on bird watching, which he is very interested in. On Mondays he goes to martial arts. On Tuesdays he goes to book club. On Wednesdays he goes to rock climbing. On Thursdays and Fridays he goes to guitar practice. On Saturdays and Sundays he goes to swimming. He loves all of these hobbies, but he really wants to do bird watching as well.

   _____

Name _____

Fiction
Theme

1

A **theme** is a lesson or message in a story.
The theme is about an important topic in the story.
Ask these questions to figure out the story's theme:

What problems do the characters struggle with in the story?

Do the character's actions suggest a certain theme?

Read the paragraph. Then answer the questions.

Santos went first in the skateboarding competition. When he didn't land one of his jumps correctly, he was disappointed. But he shrugged it off, hopped back on his board, and continued his routine. Chelsea skated after him. She was doing really well and landed some difficult jumps, but then she also missed a landing. She was so mad that she kicked her board across the pavement and yelled, and some people in the audience looked concerned. Santos ended up winning the competition. After the winner was announced, he gave Chelsea a high five and said, "Mistakes happen, but you skated really well. Can you teach me some of those tricks?" Chelsea smiled. "Congratulations on winning," she said. "I'm sorry I threw a fit. I'd love to skate with you sometime, and I'd like to learn some of your moves, too."

1. What is the theme of this story?
   Ⓐ It is much easier to be a good sport when you are the winner.
   Ⓑ Part of skateboarding is having to shake the loser's hand.
   Ⓒ Part of being good at sports is practicing good sportsmanship.
   Ⓓ Skateboarding has competitions, but it's not a real sport.

2. How do Santos's actions relate to the theme?

   _____

   _____

3. How do Chelsea's actions relate to the theme?

   _____

   _____

Name _____

Fiction

Theme

2

> A **theme** is a lesson or message in a story.
> The theme is about an important topic in the story.
>
> These are some common theme topics:
>
> | honesty | friendship | bravery |
> |---|---|---|
> | perseverance | hard work | believing in yourself |

Read the paragraph. Then circle the theme topic that goes with it.

1. Francesca's dad is a jogger. He runs every morning. He also eats nutritious foods. Francesca's dad cooks nutritious meals for Francesca and her sister. He encourages them to eat nutritious snacks and to exercise daily. He lets Francesca and her sister have junk food sometimes, but he says that they should have it rarely because it's not very good for them. Francesca eats lots of vegetables because she likes them and they're always in the fridge at her house. Soon, she wants to start jogging with her dad.

    making healthy choices   listening to your parents

Read the paragraph. Then circle the theme that goes with it.

2. The best gift that Zia ever got was a remote control car. He got it last year for his birthday. It was red, and it could reverse and move at five different speeds. It didn't look so red anymore, though, because Zia had played with it so much, making it do flips and wheelies. Lately, Zia wasn't playing with his car at all. He couldn't take his eyes off the new flying drone plane that his older brother, Mike, got for his birthday. In fact, Zia felt annoyed every time he saw Mike playing with it. "Why should he get one of those and not me?" he kept thinking. One day, Zia even thought about breaking the drone plane. "That would serve Mike right for flying it in front of me," he thought. It got to the point that Zia was hardly eating or sleeping. He was just thinking about the drone plane. Zia's mom thought that he might be sick because he wasn't eating.

    It is better to focus on what you have instead of what others have.

    Decide for yourself what is right and what is wrong.

The Crane Wife

There was once a poor sailmaker named Tashiki. He worked very hard every day, but he didn't make much money. He had a roof over his head and food to eat, so he lived comfortably, although he felt lonely because he had nobody to share his simple life with.

One day, an injured crane lay near Tashiki's front steps. "Poor crane," he whispered. He carefully scooped up the crane and brought it inside. He cared for it all winter long. One day, it was strong enough to fly away. As Tashiki watched it, he thought, "If only I could capture that crane's swiftness in one of my sails."

The following spring, a beautiful woman knocked at Tashiki's door. "My name is Yukiko," she said softly. "I've been walking for several days, and I need food and rest." Tashiki invited her in and helped her. A month later, they got married.

"I can make wonderful sails for you," Yukiko said. "They will be the most beautiful sails you have ever seen, and you will make a good amount of money from them. However, you must promise to never watch me make the sails."

Tashiki said, "I promise."

Yukiko went to her weaving room. A month went by before the first sail was finished. When Tashiki finally brought it to the market, he was surprised that people wanted to pay a lot of money for it. He asked Yukiko to weave more sails. As she wove sail after sail, Tashiki's wealth grew. He spent his new fortune on fine clothing, fancy jewelry, and expensive paintings. As he made more money and got more things, he slowly became more and more greedy.

One day, Yukiko said she needed to rest. She was so exhausted. But Tashiki demanded that she keep working, so she did. She made many more sails, but Tashiki wanted her to work faster. He became impatient with Yukiko. One day, he was so furious that he forgot about the promise he'd made. He threw open the door to Yukiko's weaving room and was astonished to see a beautiful crane weaving its splendid feathers into a sail.

Tashiki gasped. "You're the crane that I saved!"

"Yes," the crane said. "But you've broken your promise, so now I have no choice but to leave."

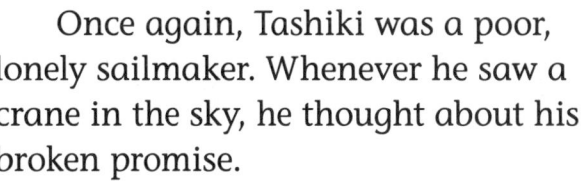

Once again, Tashiki was a poor, lonely sailmaker. Whenever he saw a crane in the sky, he thought about his broken promise.

Name _____

Fiction
Theme

The Crane Wife

3

> A **theme** is a lesson or message in a story.
> The theme is about an important topic in the story.
> Ask these questions to figure out the story's theme:
>
> What problems do the characters struggle with in the story?
>
> Do the character's actions suggest a certain theme?
>
> Do the characters learn any lessons in the story?
>
> What is important to the characters in the story?

Answer the items about the story you read.

1. **It is important to keep your promises.** Explain how this theme is shown in the story.

   _____

   _____

   _____

2. **Greed will not lead to happiness.** Explain how this theme is shown in the story.

   _____

   _____

   _____

3. How did Tashiki feel as a result of being greedy and breaking his promise?

   _____

   _____

4. Why do you think Yukiko felt like she had to leave Tashiki?

   _____

   _____

   _____

Name _____

Fiction

Theme

Review

Answer the items.

1. Explain in your own words what a theme is in a story.

   _____

   _____

2. Write four possible themes or theme topics that you can think of.

   _____   _____

   _____   _____

3. Explain how a character's actions can show the theme of a story.

   _____

   _____

   _____

4. Write a question you can ask yourself to figure out the theme of a story.

   _____

5. When a character learns a lesson in a story, do you think that readers can also learn the same lesson as they're reading? Explain your answer.

   _____

   _____

Read the paragraph. Then write what you think the theme is.

6. Mrs. Daly was an older woman who lived next door to Jen and her family. One day, Jen and her mom saw Mrs. Daly in the grocery store parking lot. Mrs. Daly was having a hard time with her grocery bag. It looked heavy and overstuffed. As Jen was about to get in the car to leave, Mrs. Daly's bag tore! Jen ran over to help Mrs. Daly pick up the oranges that had fallen onto the ground. Mrs. Daly thanked Jen a million times over the next few weeks. It warmed Jen's heart to be able to help.

   _____

Name _____

Fiction
Point of View

1

> Every story is written from the narrator's **point of view**.
>
> The **first person** point of view is when the narrator uses the word **I** or **me** to tell the story.
>
> The **second person** point of view is when the narrator uses the word **you** to tell the story.
>
> The **third person** point of view is when the narrator uses the word **he**, **she**, **it**, or **they**, or uses characters' names, to tell the story.

Read the sentence. Then write **first**, **second**, or **third** to tell the point of view it is written in.

1. Koji yawned and stretched as his alarm clock rang. _____

2. You used cinnamon-flavored toothpaste this morning. _____

3. April and Vince wake up at the same time every morning. _____

4. I stuffed a sweatshirt into my backpack. _____

5. When you get to school, you hang up your backpack. _____

6. I feel sick whenever I get egg salad in my lunch. _____

Read the paragraph. Then answer the question.

7.   Alvin follows the same routine almost every morning. The first thing he does after he gets out of bed is brush his teeth and wash his face. After that, he gets dressed. Then, he combs his hair. Most mornings, Alvin has toast or cereal for breakfast. After eating, he gets his school materials ready and packed up in his backpack. Then he gives his mom a kiss on the cheek before he walks to the school bus. Of course, his routine is a little bit different on weekend mornings, when he doesn't go to school.

What point of view is the paragraph written in? Explain how you know.

_____

_____

_____

Name _____

Fiction
Point of View

2

The narrator gives the story its **point of view**. Point of view is the way in which the story is seen and told. A story can be told in the **first person**, **second person**, or **third person** point of view.

When you read a story told in the first or third person point of view, ask whether or not the narrator is **omniscient** or **limited**.

An **omniscient** narrator knows everything about the story. The narrator knows what all the characters think, feel, and plan to do. The narrator often knows what will happen later.

A **limited** narrator has limited knowledge about the story. The narrator knows only what the main character thinks, feels, and plans to do, but not the other characters. The narrator often does not know what will happen later.

Read the paragraph. Then answer the items.

Lakwonda's little sister, Cynthia, asked for help with her homework, and Lakwonda immediately agreed to help, even though she had her own homework assignment to work on. If only Lakwonda knew that she was going to be helping Cynthia the entire night, she may not have agreed to help at all. Cynthia's homework assignment was actually a big book report that was due the next day. By the time Lakwonda was finished helping her sister, it was 10 o'clock at night, and Lakwonda still had her own homework to finish. Lakwonda was exhausted and frustrated, but she didn't show it. And her help meant so much that Cynthia never forgot it, even as an adult.

1. Is the paragraph written in the third person omniscient or limited point of view? Explain why you think so.

_____

_____

2. The narrator writes, "If Lakwonda only knew that she was going to be helping Cynthia the entire night, she may not have agreed." This shows that _____.

   Ⓐ Cynthia will not appreciate Lakwonda's help later on
   Ⓑ Lakwonda did not have to help Cynthia for very long
   Ⓒ the story will end before we find out what the narrator means
   Ⓓ the narrator knows what will happen later in the story

Mary's Independence Day

June 29, 1874

Dear Diary,

This week, the shoe cobbler rode his wagon to our farm. I'm so glad he did because my shabby old shoes were getting too small! Ma, Pa, and my little brother Zack got new shoes, too. It had been a year since the shoe cobbler came by the last time. He'll make our new shoes at his shop and bring them by our farm when they're done. I sure do hope they'll be ready by Independence Day.

June 30, 1874

Independence Day is getting closer, so we're going into town for the celebration. Ma's baking gooseberry pies, so Zack and I spent the day picking berries, pumping water from the well, and getting firewood for the stove.

July 1, 1874

Last year on Independence Day, Hattie Johnson and her five sisters wore matching dresses that their Ma had sewn. Boys teased them all for looking identical, but Hattie smiled and giggled. I don't know for certain if Hattie felt bad when the boys teased her, but, as far as I could tell, she loved being the center of attention. I hope my new shoes get here soon, because those boys will tease me if I'm still wearing my shabby old ones, and I don't want the attention!

July 2, 1874

Pa says they're holding a mud race again this year. Anyone from our town can race in the mud, but it sure is messy! Last year, our neighbor Big Joe won, and afterward, he hugged his wife, still covered from head to toe in mud. She took off running and screaming. Now, that was hysterical! I wonder who will win the race this year.

July 3, 1874

The cobbler brought my new shoes today, and they sure do look spiffy! I wasn't sure that they would be done in time, but I have them now.

July 5, 1874

I didn't write yesterday because it was Independence Day. I spent most of the day with Hattie. After the parade, the mayor made a speech. Then all the town folk headed to the field where the fiddlers played. Just about everybody in town danced, including Ma and Pa. I even danced with Hattie! It was the best Independence Day yet!

Name _____

Fiction
Point of View

3

Mary's Independence Day

A story can be told in the **first person**, **second person**, or **third person** point of view. Think about whether the narrator's knowledge is **omniscient** or **limited**.

Ask these questions as you read:

>   Whose thoughts do you read in the story?
>
>   Whose feelings or plans does the narrator describe?
>
>   Is the narrator a character in the story?
>
>   Are there things that the narrator does not know or is uncertain about?

Answer the items about the story you read.

1. Is the story told in the first, second, or third person point of view? Explain your answer.

   _____

   _____

2. Describe the narrator. Explain who the narrator is.

   _____

   _____

3. Is the narrator's knowledge omniscient or limited? Explain why you think so.

   _____

   _____

4. Write two things that Mary is uncertain about in the story.

   _____

   _____

   _____

Name _____

Fiction
Point of View

Review

Answer the item.

1. Mark the sentence that is written from the second person point of view.
   - Ⓐ Megan has to finish her project tonight.
   - Ⓑ Aisha is doing research at the library.
   - Ⓒ The loud noises are distracting you as you try to study.
   - Ⓓ I have to get some art supplies to finish this project.

Read the sentence. Then write **first**, **second**, or **third** to tell the point of view in which it is written.

2. I thought I saw a dark shadow move in the hallway. _____

3. Loretta thinks the doll in the attic is creepy. _____

4. You never go into the dark, cold basement. _____

Read the paragraph. Then answer the questions.

   I am so excited for tonight that I can't sit still. Tonight, my whole family will be at my house, and I will be able to open all of my birthday presents. My sister, Anya, has been telling me for two whole days that there is a big surprise waiting for me. I keep trying to guess what the surprise is. Whenever Anya seems like she will break down and tell me, she starts laughing nervously and runs away. "I can't ruin the surprise!" she yells each time. I finally realized that I'll just have to wait until tonight to find out what the surprise is.

5. What point of view is the story written in? Explain how you know.

   _____
   _____
   _____

6. What additional information would we know if Anya were the narrator of this story instead of this narrator? Explain why you think so.

   _____
   _____
   _____

Name _____

Fiction
Vocabulary
1

When you read, you may come across unfamiliar **vocabulary**, or words, that you don't know. When you come to a word you don't know the meaning of, try this:

Look at the surrounding words. Think about what would make sense in the sentence.

Think about what you know about the topic.

Read the sentence before the word. Read the sentence after the word.

Read the paragraph. Using context clues, fill in the blanks with words from the word bank.

1. | demonstrate   ancestors   fragile   segment |

   Mohammed's class went on a field trip to the museum. The tour guide told them not to touch anything. "These objects are _____," she said. "They can break easily." She then showed the students a _____ from a cave painting. It was not the entire painting, just a small piece. It showed a man hunting a wild animal. The tour guide said that early humans made the painting. "Those early humans are our _____," she said. "We have the technology and skills that we have today because these early people learned what works and what doesn't work. And, these paintings _____ the great skills they had—not just in painting, but in hunting, too."

Read the paragraph. Then answer the item.

2. Zeke had only ever seen a royal crown in the movies. He had never seen an **authentic** one, worn by an actual king, before he went to the museum last week. Apparently, it had been worn by King Meetrius in the year 1600.

Using information from the text, explain what the word **authentic** means.

_____

© Evan-Moor Corp. • EMC 2424 • Reading Comprehension Fundamentals

115

The Robotics Wizard

Kiara was looking forward to the start of the school year because she'd just moved to town in August, and with half the town's population on vacation, she hadn't met a single kid yet. Sure, the first day of school meant the start of homework and tests and book reports, but there was also the possibility of meeting new friends.

A few days into school, Kiara brought home information on the fall clubs the school was offering.

"Robotics Club," Kiara's dad said as he looked at the paper. "You love that kind of stuff, Kiara. Let's sign you up."

Kiara agreed, but she was apprehensive. Sure, she liked robotics and technology, but she was sure that most kids knew a lot more about those topics than she did. Would she fit in?

On the first day of Robotics Club, Kiara walked quietly into the classroom and sat next to a couple of kids she recognized from class.

Mr. Taylor, the teacher, talked about how robots are used. "Robots work in factories, manufacturing all sorts of things," he said, "like cars, airplane parts, and even things you might not expect, like pancakes!"

Mr. Taylor then explained that many industries were becoming automated. "That means robots are replacing human workers," the teacher said. "Robots can be programmed to perform tasks quickly and precisely, without making mistakes. Does anyone know where else robots are used?"

Kiara raised her hand. "They're used for space exploration," she said. "Outer space can be hazardous for humans since there's lots of harmful radiation and no air. Those things don't matter to robots, though."

"Very good!" Mr. Taylor said. "Today we're going to make a very basic robot, called a bristlebot," Mr. Taylor said. "Does anyone have any previous experience with them?"

Kiara raised her hand. "Yes, I've made them before. You just need a toothbrush, a cell battery, a small motor with two wires, and some tape."

As the teacher pulled items from a plastic tub, a boy leaned over to Kiara.

"How do you know so much about robots?" he asked. "You're like a robotics wizard," he said.

As Kiara worked with her group, she realized she'd found a great club to join—and a great group of friends, too!

Name _____

Fiction
Vocabulary

2

The Robotics Wizard

> When we talk about **vocabulary** in a story, we refer to all of the words that appear in the story. When you read a word you don't know, you can use context clues to figure out its meaning.
>
> Ask the following questions as you read:
>
> What is the subject of the story?
>
> Do any other words or phrases give clues to the word's meaning?
>
> Can I replace this word with another word I know that may have a similar meaning?

Answer the items about the text you read.

1. Using context clues, explain what *apprehensive* means.

   _____

   _____

   _____

2. What details in the story tell you that *hazardous* means "dangerous"?

   _____

   _____

3. How can you tell that *previous* means something happened before?

   _____

   _____

   _____

4. Find words in the story that you didn't know. Pick one, look up the definition, and then write it down.

   _____

   _____

Name _____

Fiction

Vocabulary

Review

Answer the item.

1. Write two things you can do if you come across an unfamiliar word.

_____

_____

_____

Read the paragraph. Then answer the item.

2.   When Angela drank the last of the milk, I thought she was being selfish. But then I found out that she had poured it into a saucer for a homeless cat that appeared in our yard. I was glad that she had used the last of the milk for such a noble reason.

The word *noble* probably means _____.

Ⓐ moral and good
Ⓑ selfish and rude
Ⓒ questionable
Ⓓ strange

3.   Uncle Paco always tells jokes. Yesterday, he told the whole family a joke, and everyone laughed. Everyone except Ana, that is. Ana did not understand the joke at all. She frowned when everyone else laughed. So Uncle Paco repeated the joke to her. She still didn't understand what was so hilarious. Finally, Ana wrote down the joke so that she could read it slowly and analyze it. Ana divided the joke into separate sentences. She read each part slowly and repeated it. There was one word that she had to look up the meaning for. After she analyzed the joke, she finally understood why everyone was laughing.

What does the word *analyze* mean? Explain how you know.

_____

_____

_____

_____

Name _____

Fiction
Visual Information

1

Many stories include **visual information**, such as illustrations.

Visual information can help you to better understand the story.

Visual information can show details that aren't provided in the text.

Read the paragraph and look at the picture. Then finish the sentence.

1. Ronny and his dad wandered around the museum. They had seen many different exhibits. Now, they were at Ronny's favorite exhibit.

    Ronny's favorite museum exhibit is the _____ exhibit.
    - Ⓐ wild animal
    - Ⓑ art
    - Ⓒ mummy
    - Ⓓ dinosaur

Read the paragraph and look at the picture. Then answer the question.

2. Anita went on a field trip to the museum with her class. She got to see statues, paintings, and mummies. She decided that she wanted to bring something home from the museum so that she could always remember the field trip. After all, her mom had given her some money to spend.

What part of the museum is Anita in? Explain how you know.

_____

_____

_____

Harvest Season on Phebos

On Saturday, Tan and I woke up early, well before the suns peeked above the horizon. Tan is my older brother, and it's up to the two of us to help Mom around the farm right now because Dad is traveling on another planet for work. After a quick breakfast, Mom got the hover-barrow from the barn, and the three of us walked out to the fields.

"Today is going to be great!" I said. Despite all the chores we had to do, I loved harvest season. I loved the feeling of cooler temperatures and the change of colors in the trees. My teacher said that harvest season on Phebos is similar to that on Earth, where many people originally came from. Well, I didn't come from there. I was born right here on Phebos. But Mom says that my great-grandparents used to live there. My best friend, Zelly, has a grandfather who used to live on Earth a long time ago. When I'm over at her house, he tells us stories about it. "Back on Earth, harvest season was really hard work," he'd say. "We didn't have any easy hover-barrows to use. We put our crops in wheelbarrows, which we had to push around on the ground."

Anyway, the biggest reason I love harvest season is because the rizzmargles are finally ripe and ready for picking. I mean, who doesn't love rizzmargle pie? It's the perfect combination of sweet and sour.

When we got to the field, Mom groaned. "Oh, no! The chippets have gotten into the rizzmargle patch again," she said. We spotted a line of tiny animal tracks leading directly into the rizzmargle patch. Luckily for us, only one chippet came into the patch, and it was still there! "Shoo!" yelled Tan, scaring the chippet away.

We still had plenty of rizzmargles left in the patch. Tan and I started picking ripe rizzmargles and piling them into the hover-barrow. Mom fixed the hole in the fence. After a while, my arms started to get tired from lifting so many rizzmargles. They're heavier than they look! And, Tan and I felt hot from all the suns beating down on us. When the hover-barrow was full, we all headed back to the farmhouse.

Name _____

Harvest Season on Phebos

Fiction
Visual Information

2

> Many stories include **visual information**, such as illustrations. Visual information can help you to better understand the story. Ask these questions as you read:
>
> Do the pictures show details that aren't provided in the text?
>
> Do the pictures show details about the setting or the characters?

Answer the items about the story you read.

1. Write three things shown in the picture that Earth does not have.

   _____

   _____

   _____

2. Look at the picture. What animal from Earth do chippets remind you of? Explain why you think so.

   _____

3. Which detail is shown in the picture but not provided in the story's text?
   - Ⓐ A wheelbarrow floats through the air.
   - Ⓑ A hover-barrow gets pushed on the ground.
   - Ⓒ A hover-barrow floats through the air.
   - Ⓓ Phebos has wheelbarrows but not hover-barrows.

4. Why do you think that Zelly's grandfather calls hover-barrows "easy" to use compared to wheelbarrows?

   _____

   _____

5. What crop from Earth do rizzmargles remind you of? Explain why you think so.

   _____

   _____

© Evan-Moor Corp. • EMC 2424 • Reading Comprehension Fundamentals

Name _____

Fiction

Visual Information

Review

Read the paragraph and look at the picture. Then answer the question.

1.   Giada and her dad like spending time together. Yesterday was Friday, and they went to see a movie at the theater. Today they are doing the same thing they do every Saturday.

   What do Giada and her dad do every Saturday?

   _____

2.   Velma and her brother are going to walk to the park together. Velma waits for her brother on the front porch. She really wants him to hurry. "Come on, Jonah!" she yells. Velma is feeling more uncomfortable as she stands still on the porch. "Why can't Jonah just hurry?" she wonders as she takes a deep breath.

   Why does Velma want Jonah to hurry so much?

   _____

3.   Patrick's dad felt unhappy. "I don't have nearly enough time to do all the yard work that needs to get done today," he complained. "I have to water the flowers, replant the trees, and trim the bushes." Patrick decided to help his dad.

   How does Patrick help his dad?

   _____

Answer the item.

4. Describe the kinds of details that visual information can give you as you read a story.

   _____

   _____

   _____

Name _____

Fiction

Summarize

1

When you **summarize** a story, you use your own words to state the most important details from the story. A **summary** is always shorter than the story. These are some details you can include in a summary:

| who the main characters are | what problem the characters have |
| how the characters feel | how the characters solve the problem |

Read the paragraph. Then summarize what you read.

1. Lola was busy today. She woke up at 6 o'clock in the morning to get ready for school, ate breakfast, and walked to the bus stop. At school, Lola's teacher asked the students for their signed permission slips for the field trip next week. Lola had forgotten to ask her mom to sign the permission slip! Lola's teacher said that today was the last day to turn in permission slips, so Lola had to go to the office at recess to call her mom. Lola's mom dropped off the permission slip at the end of the school day. Then she drove Lola to rock climbing. Lola did rock climbing until 6:30. She didn't get to eat dinner until 7 o'clock. By 8 o'clock, she was yawning and ready for bed.

   _____
   _____
   _____
   _____

2. Kody worked hard on the poster for his science presentation. He was going to show it as he gave his speech in front of the class. He carefully put the poster on the car seat next to him and held it in place on the drive to school. When he got out of the car, he said goodbye to his dad and shut the car door. As soon as his dad drove away, Kody felt a moment of panic. He realized that he had forgotten his poster in the car!

   _____
   _____

My Adventure with Sidney

I love my older sister, Sidney. She goes to college. Even though she is so much older than I am, we love spending time together. Last week, though, we had an unusual experience together.

Sidney had come home to visit for a few days. One afternoon, I had to go to soccer practice at 5 o'clock. Dad couldn't take me because he had to work, so Sidney said that she would drive me. Soccer practice was being held at Walker Park, a new park on the other side of town, and neither Sidney nor I knew how to get there. Sidney said that we could use the map on her phone to find it.

While Sidney drove, I used her phone to look at the map. We had been on the road for five minutes when Sidney's phone made a loud beeping sound.

"Uh-oh," I said, "the battery is not charged. I think it's going out." Then the phone beeped again. Then it was off.

Sidney said that she didn't have her power cord with her. "It's okay, Andrea," she said. "I looked at the map before we left the house, and I think I know how to get to the park."

The sun was starting to set, so the sunlight was getting a little dimmer. I must have looked nervous because Sidney said, "We'll find it, don't worry!"

Sidney turned left on Parker Lane. Then she turned right on Grover Street. She stopped at two stop signs. Then I noticed the time on the car's clock. It was 5:05 p.m. I was already late to soccer practice. But that didn't worry me as much as the darkening sky.

"It's okay, you'll only be a few minutes late," said Sidney. I think she was getting a little nervous, too.

After ten minutes and a few more turns, we found ourselves on Fang Road. It was now pretty dark, and this was a part of town where we had never been before. And this road was kind of creepy, too. Sidney stopped at a red light. "Um, I think the park is up ahead, on the right," she said slowly. We waited and waited. But the light didn't turn green! There were no other cars around, either. "I wonder if this traffic light is broken," I said. We waited some more.

After we had spent seven whole minutes stopped at the red light, it finally turned green. I laughed and said, "I think I'll just go home and explain to Coach next week why I couldn't make it to practice."

Sidney laughed, too. Then she got really serious and gulped. "Now we just have to find our way home."

Name _____

My Adventure with Sidney

When you **summarize** a story, you use your own words to state the most important details from the story. When you summarize, it shows that you understand what happened in the story. Include these details in a summary:

- who the main characters are
- what the characters do
- where and when the story happens
- what problem the characters have

Answer the items about the story you read.

1. Who are the main characters in the story?

   _____   _____

2. Describe where and when the story happens.

   _____
   _____

3. Describe Sidney and Andrea's relationship with each other.

   _____
   _____

4. Summarize the story.

   _____
   _____
   _____
   _____
   _____
   _____
   _____

Fiction
Summarize

2

Name _____

Fiction

Summarize

Review

Answer the items.

1. A summary is _____.
   - Ⓐ always longer than the text you are summarizing
   - Ⓑ when you retell the whole story and include all the details
   - Ⓒ always shorter than the text you are summarizing
   - Ⓓ a short story

2. Explain what a summary is.

   _____

   _____

3. Write two details that you can include in a summary of a story.

   _____

   _____

Read the paragraphs. Then summarize what you read.

4.   Paul and his dad were riding their bikes on a hill when they heard a growl. Paul's dad thought that the sound might have come from a mountain lion. He told Paul to stay still. Paul's dad took his keys out of his pocket and starting jingling them. "If we make ourselves really big and loud, we may scare off the mountain lion."

   Paul was laughing so hard that he couldn't stand up straight. Finally, he was able to say a few words through the laughter. "Dad, it wasn't a mountain lion," he said. "That was my tummy! I'm starving."

   "But it was so loud!" said Paul's dad. He smiled, and he felt silly.

   _____

   _____

   _____

   _____

Name _____

Fiction

Make Inferences

1

> As you read a story, you can **make inferences** to better understand it. When you make an inference, you use what you know and clues in the story to figure out something that is not directly stated.
>
> Here is an example of an inference:
>
> **I read:** Every time Tana gets ready to leave her house, her dog Buck whines. He looks at his leash by the door, and then he looks at Tana.
>
> **I make this inference:** Buck wants to go with Tana.

Read the paragraph. Then circle the sentence that tells the inference you can make about what you read.

1. When Dylan saw a big dog, he grew quiet. The dog wagged its tail. Dylan took a careful step backward.

   Dylan loves dogs.   Dylan is nervous around dogs.

2. Margo's dog is named Lula. When Lula was younger, she could go on long walks with Margo. Lula is 14 years old now.

   Lula can't go on long walks.   Lula goes on long walks.

3. Sometimes mice run into our house. Our dog Snow can sniff out any mouse. Snow has found mice under our fridge, behind our sofa, and between our bookshelves. Yesterday, Snow started sniffing around in the kitchen.

   Snow smelled a mouse behind the sofa.   Snow smelled a mouse in the kitchen.

Read the paragraph. Then write one inference you can make about what you read.

4. Bart's dog Noodle leaves fur everywhere! When Noodle gets on the couch, the cushions are covered in golden fur. When Noodle rolls on the carpet, a layer of golden fur is left behind. This morning, Bart found a heap of golden fur on his bed!

   _____

A New Park

"Giang! Time to get in the car!"

Groaning loudly, Giang dragged his feet downstairs and made his way to the front door. Before he stepped out, he looked wishfully at the TV. Normally, Giang would sleep late on Saturdays and then watch his favorite shows. But today was different. Giang's mom had volunteered to do some outdoor work, and she was making him go with her.

Giang's mom was a member of a land conservation group. Their goal was to help wildlife and people in the community by transforming lands that had been neglected and polluted with trash into community parks and trails.

Today, the group was cleaning up an area of land that would become Heron Park. This land had been polluted by people for years. The group was going to pick up garbage, post signs, and clear a trail so that visitors would know that this land was now a protected park. Anyone caught littering at the park would be breaking the law and could get into trouble.

Several people were already there when Giang and his mom arrived. Giang saw kids and adults picking up trash and posting signs.

He noticed a group standing around one man who wore a cap. The man's badge said "Roger," and people were asking him what jobs they should do. Giang's mom went to ask Roger what job she and Giang should do. "That man must be in charge," thought Giang. Soon, Giang and his mom were clearing garbage from an old trail.

Giang got to check out Heron Park as he worked, and it was beautiful. It had grass and hills. It had a creek. Giang saw lots of birds. And he was excited when he saw a deer. He had never had so much fun doing work on a Saturday before, and he didn't even miss the TV!

Name _____

Fiction

Make Inferences

2

A New Park

As you read a story, you can **make inferences** to better understand it. When you make an inference, you use what you know and clues in the story to figure out something that is not directly stated.

You can use **pictures** and **words** to make inferences.

Answer the items about the story you read.

1. Before Giang saw Heron Park, what did he want to spend his Saturday doing? Explain why you think so.

   _____
   _____

2. Why do you think that the conservation group felt that they needed to protect the land at Heron Park? Use details from the story to explain your answer.

   _____
   _____

3. Why would littering at the park be breaking the law?

   _____
   _____

4. Why did Giang think Roger was in charge of cleaning up the park? Explain why you think so.

   _____
   _____

5. Explain why Giang didn't miss the TV.

   _____

Name _____

Fiction
Make Inferences

Review

Answer the items.

1. When you make an inference about a story, you _____.
   - Ⓐ read about something that the author wrote
   - Ⓑ figure out something that is not directly stated
   - Ⓒ do research to find out more about the story's subject
   - Ⓓ look for certain words and phrases in the story

2. Explain how you make inferences when you read.

   _____
   _____

Read the paragraph. Then answer the question.

3.   Corbin's first day at his new school went great. When his classmate Thalia showed him around the school, she told him that the school buses leave the school at 3:15 in the afternoon, sharp, every day. "Oh, that's okay," said Corbin, "I'm a walker." Later, after the final bell rang, Corbin stayed behind for a little while to talk to his teacher. When he finally left, he saw a boy from another class running down the hallway with his backpack. The boy looked worried. A few minutes later, Corbin saw the same boy, along with a few other kids, standing in a line outside of the school office. Corbin noticed that the time was 3:20.

   Why are students lining up outside the school office? Explain why you think so.

   _____
   _____
   _____

Read the paragraph. Then write one inference you can make. Explain why you made this inference.

4.   On Monday, Niko bought a new box of rice crackers. It had ten packets. He asked his siblings not to eat his rice crackers. On Friday, Niko saw three packets of rice crackers in the trash can. He saw rice cracker crumbs on the floor.

   _____
   _____

Name _____

Fiction

Predict

1

You can **predict** as you read a story. When you predict, you use clues in the story to think about what will happen later.

These are some story clues that can help you predict:

character traits

things characters have said or done

things that can cause a problem later on in the story

Read the paragraph. Then answer the item.

1. Pablo is extremely organized. He keeps all of his school materials well organized, and his teachers know that he loves to help make things neat. In gym class, he helped the teacher organize the shed with all the sports equipment. When he volunteered in the school cafeteria, he helped the school cook to organize the serving spoons. Today Pablo is in art class, and he has noticed that the art supply drawers are messy. There are markers in the paintbrush drawer and pastels in the crayon drawer.

Predict what Pablo will do in art class today. Explain why you think so.

_____

_____

Read the paragraph. Then answer the item.

2. Hewot's teacher assigned a project to the class. They had two weeks to complete it. She gave the students the choice to work alone or in a group, and she said that they had one week to decide. Hewot was a very dedicated student, and she usually chose to work alone. But this time she thought it would be fun to work in a group, so she asked Wynn, Sam, and Luiz to work with her. As they began working together, Wynn was goofing off. Sam was being bossy and trying to do most of the project himself. Luiz was disagreeing with all of Hewot's ideas. Hewot wanted to do a good job and to have the teacher notice her work on the project.

Predict what you think Hewot will do by the end of the first week.

_____

_____

The High School Play

My older brother, Lars, has the lead role in the high school play on Friday night. Lars' entire life seems to be about theater because he loves acting and singing. He says that theater is his favorite thing to do. Next year, he's going to college in the city to study acting. One day, he hopes to be a professional actor.

Even though Lars loves being on stage, he's been extremely nervous for the past few weeks. He can hardly eat, and he stays up late each night rehearsing his lines over and over again. He won't even eat before rehearsals. Mom tried to drop off some spaghetti to him after school one day before rehearsal, and he said, "I can't eat this now because I'll feel sick." He said he'd eat dinner later after he got home.

I think I know why Lars has been so nervous. Last year, he had a big role in a musical, and he forgot one of his lines while he was on stage.

It wasn't a big deal. I don't think the audience even noticed that he forgot a line because he knew how to stall for a second while another actor whispered the line to him. After the show, though, Lars was miserable because of his mistake, and now he may be worried that it'll happen again.

Every time Lars has a show, we do certain things to celebrate. We always get roses to throw up on stage after the show has ended and the actors have bowed. We also wait in the school lobby for all the actors to come out in costume. We get to take pictures with them and tell them how much we enjoyed their performances and costumes.

Dad suggested we go out to dinner Friday night, to celebrate Lars' lead role. After all, this will be Lars' last time performing in a high school play because he will graduate from high school soon. Dad and Mom couldn't decide if we should eat before the play or after. We might feel rushed if we eat before the play, but if we wait until after, we'll be eating pretty late. I don't care either way. It'll be Friday night, so I won't have to wake up early the next morning. Mom and Dad finally just decided to ask Lars on Friday whether he prefers to eat dinner before or after the play.

On Thursday evening, Mom ordered a dozen roses from a flower shop online. Then I heard her say to my dad, "Honey, make sure you charge the digital camera tonight!" I think Friday night will be fun.

Name _____

Fiction

Predict

2

The High School Play

You can **predict** as you read a story. When you make predictions, you are looking closely at the story's details to think about what will happen later.

These are some things you can predict in a story:

- problems that will arise
- how characters will solve problems
- things the characters will choose to do

Answer the items about the story you read.

1. Predict how you think Lars will perform in the play. Explain why you think so.

   _____
   _____
   _____

2. Predict what Lars will do if he forgets a line when he's on stage.

   _____
   _____

3. Predict whether Lars will want to eat before or after the play on Friday. Explain why you think so.

   _____
   _____
   _____

4. Predict what Mom will do with the roses and camera.

   _____
   _____

© Evan-Moor Corp. • EMC 2424 • Reading Comprehension Fundamentals

Name _____

Fiction
Predict

Review

Answer the items.

1. Explain how details about character traits can help you make predictions about a story.

   _____
   _____

2. How can you use details to predict problems that may arise later in the story?

   _____
   _____
   _____

3. When a character deals with a problem, does this help you predict how the character will solve problems later on? Explain why you think so.

   _____
   _____

4. Write one thing that you can make a prediction about in a story.

   _____
   _____

Read the paragraph. Then answer the item.

5.   Wanda receives a weekly allowance of five dollars and is always looking for ways to make extra money. She told her dad that she'd do the dishes after dinner for an extra fifty cents. She told her mom that she would give the dog a bath for an extra two dollars. She told her little sister that she'd braid her hair for a quarter. She told her grandma that she'd make her some buttered toast for seventy-five cents. Yesterday, Wanda heard her parents tell Chester, her brother, that he had to clean his room. When Wanda had a chance, she knocked on Chester's door to talk to him.

   Predict what you think Wanda wants to talk to Chester about. Explain why you think so.

   _____
   _____

Name _____

Fiction

Cause and Effect

1

> You can consider **cause and effect** as you read a story. When you think about cause and effect, it helps you understand why certain events happen in the story. Ask the following questions as you read:
>
> What effect does the setting or environment have on a character's actions?
>
> Do a character's actions cause something else to happen?
>
> How does an event in the story cause a character to feel?

Read the paragraphs. Then answer the item.

1.   Bilal was at his after-school running club. At first, he didn't think he'd like running, but he joined because his dad was a runner. It had rained the night before, so the trails were muddy. Bilal's friend Jake slipped, but he got ahold of his footing and kept running. Bilal, meanwhile, felt exhausted. He just wanted to take a break even though he knew he should push himself to keep going. "There's a 5K race next week," Jake said. "I'm going to participate. You should do it with me."
    Suddenly, Bilal imagined himself running in the 5K race, and he instantly had more energy. "I'll definitely do that!" he said.

Draw a line to match each cause to an effect.

cause	**effect**
Bilal's dad was a runner. ●	● Bilal had more energy.
It rained the night before. ●	● Bilal decided to join the running club.
Jake mentioned the 5K race. ●	● The trails were muddy, and Jake slipped.

Read the paragraph. Then write one possible effect of the runners' actions.

2.   The coach told the runners to pace themselves. If they didn't run very fast at the start, then they wouldn't become exhausted too quickly, and they would be able to finish the whole run. But all of the runners ran as fast as they could at the start.

_____

_____

Flying Turtle: A Lakota Folktale

Turtle loved to talk, and he loved eating leaves. Now that it was autumn, he had lots of food because the leaves would fall from the trees. One day, as Turtle was munching on a leaf, he saw a group of birds squawking excitedly.

"Hi, Turtle!" one bird squawked. "We're getting ready to fly south."

The bird explained that winter was coming, which meant there wouldn't be much to eat. The birds were flying south, where there was always plenty of food. That sounded wonderful to Turtle. Sure, he loved autumn, but he certainly didn't like the freezing temperatures and snow that winter brought. When Turtle asked if he could go with the birds on their journey, they laughed hysterically.

"Turtles can't fly!" one bird chirped.

"Please!" Turtle said. "There must be some way that you can bring me along."

"Absolutely not," the birds cawed.

Day after day, Turtle begged and pleaded, until finally the birds agreed.

One bird had a plan. Turtle would hold a stick with his mouth while two birds held each end of the stick. This way, they could carry Turtle.

"But remember," the bird warned, "you must not let go of the stick while we're in the air!"

Soon Turtle was soaring over the trees, rivers, and mountains. The sights amazed him because he had only ever seen things from the ground.

It wasn't long before Turtle began to have lots of questions about the journey. He wanted to talk to the birds. He wondered how long the journey would take. Knowing he couldn't talk, he tried to get the birds' attention by rolling his eyes. That didn't work, so he tried flaring his nostrils and wiggling his tail. He waved his legs. Still, the birds didn't notice him. "These birds should realize how hard it is when you can't talk!" he thought angrily. Finally, Turtle lost his temper and opened his mouth to yell.

Instantly, he fell to the ground below. Crack! Turtle's shell now had cracks all over it. Aching, he plunked into a pond and buried himself in the mud at the bottom. By the time he awoke, winter had passed, and spring had arrived.

All of the turtles that came after Turtle looked the same. And, to this day, turtle shells look as if they're cracked.

Name _____

Fiction
Cause and Effect

2

Flying Turtle: A Lakota Folktale

Cause and effect helps to create an interesting plot in a story. When something happens in a story, it can cause other things to happen as a result. The plot of a story is made up of a long line of events that happen for a reason.

Answer the questions about the story you read.

1. How does the approach of winter lead Turtle to join the birds on their journey?

   _____
   _____
   _____

2. How does Turtle's love of talking cause him to lose his temper?

   _____
   _____

3. What happened as a result of Turtle losing his temper?

   _____
   _____

4. According to the folktale, what caused all turtle shells to appear cracked?

   _____
   _____

5. In your opinion, would the bird's plan to carry Turtle have worked if Turtle didn't like to talk so much? Explain why you think so.

   _____
   _____

© Evan-Moor Corp. • EMC 2424 • Reading Comprehension Fundamentals

Name _____

Fiction

Cause and Effect

Review

Answer the items.

1. Mark the sentence that tells a cause and an effect.
   - Ⓐ Paiton wore gloves, a scarf, and a coat.
   - Ⓑ Paiton wore gloves, so her hands stayed warm.
   - Ⓒ Paiton's hands are always cold.
   - Ⓓ Paiton has purple gloves, and Ray has black ones.

2. Explain how causes and effects help to create an interesting plot in a story.

   _____

   _____

   _____

3. Explain how the environment in a story can cause characters to do certain things.

   _____

   _____

   _____

Read the paragraph. Then write one cause and one effect that you read.

4.   Rhonda's older brother, Mario, was frustrated with her. Rhonda had woken Mario up at 2 o'clock in the morning the past two nights because she was thirsty. To get a glass of water, she had to walk down the long hallway to the kitchen, but she was afraid to do it alone. Why? She had watched a scary movie on Saturday when she was at her friend's sleepover. Mario agreed to walk with her two times. But on the second night, he said, "No more, Rhonda. You're on your own."

   Cause: _____

   Effect: _____

Name _____

Fiction

Compare and Contrast

1

You can use details and pictures in a story to **compare and contrast** elements of the story. For example, you can compare and contrast characters, settings, or events.

When you compare and contrast characters, look at these details:

- how the characters feel
- how the characters look
- what the characters say
- what the characters do

Read the paragraph. Then answer the item.

1. Gabrielle's class had to do book reports. She read a book about a pirate named Lazy Pete. She started reading the book right away, taking notes as she read. Lazy Pete was always getting into trouble. He constantly forgot to do his chores, like mopping the deck and putting away the ropes. His ship was quite messy. "I don't like working!" he grumbled to the captain one day. Gabrielle loved the book. When she was done, she typed up her report, made some revisions, and checked her spelling. She wanted to make sure it was perfect before she handed it in.

   In your own words, contrast Gabrielle with the character she read about, Lazy Pete.

   _____

   _____

   _____

2. Chuck and Don both turned in their book reports on time. When their teacher, Mr. King, saw Chuck's report, he smiled and nodded. But he frowned when he saw Don's report. Mr. King said, "Don, we talked about the quality of your work last time you turned in an assignment," he said.

   Explain how Chuck and Don approach schoolwork differently.

   _____

   _____

Interstellar Pen-Pals

Today was exciting because I received a coded message from my pen-pal Zela. She lives halfway across the galaxy, on a planet called Miranda. I've never been there, but it sounds like a nice place. The only time I've been off Arkin (my home planet) was when my class went on a field trip to one of our moons. And that barely counts because the moon is really close. The flight only took an hour, and we were back by the end of the school day.

Zela's family, on the other hand, has traveled to dozens of different planets. She's even been to an asteroid belt! Last year, Zela's family spent several months touring their solar system, and they even spent an afternoon on a comet. She said the comet was nothing like Miranda because it had a weird shape, and it didn't have any gravity. Their landing pod had special claws that dug into the comet's surface and held on. Then, when Zela and her parents went outside to explore, they needed to tie harnesses and ropes to their spacesuits so they wouldn't float away into outer space. Zela joked that they should let her little brother float away, and apparently her parents didn't think that was funny. I laughed when I read that because I have a little brother, too.

From what Zela said, I would absolutely love exploring a comet. She said that its weird shape made walking feel more like rock climbing. That's one thing that Zela and I have in common. We both love rock climbing.

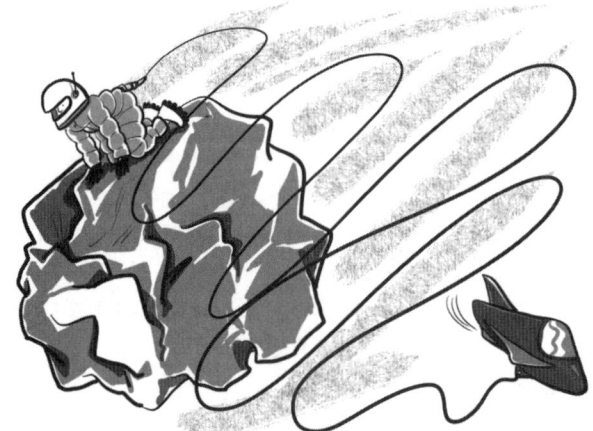

On some weekends, my family goes to a huge crater here on Arkin. Mom and my little brother hang out at the snack bar while Dad and I climb the crater's cliffs. Zela said that Miranda has craters, too, and that's where she likes to climb when she's not traveling.

Of course, we haven't been to the crater in the past couple of weeks because we just got a puppy, Dax, and he requires constant supervision. In the past week, he chewed up my favorite pair of space boots, Dad's slippers, and Mom's video phone. I suggested that Rentley, our helper robot, could take care of Dax for the day, but Mom said he's not programmed for that type of work.

Well, I'll be writing back to Zela soon, and I'm going to tell her about Dax. I know she'll want to hear about him because her family doesn't have any pets, even though she likes animals.

Name _____

Fiction
Compare and Contrast

2

Interstellar Pen-Pals

> You can **compare and contrast** two things in a story. Look for details in the story that tell about similarities and differences. Look at these kinds of details in a story:
>
> - how different characters act
> - what the pictures show
> - what different settings look like
> - how different events affect a story

Answer the items about the story you read.

1. Write three things that the narrator and Zela have in common.

   _____

   _____

   _____

2. Write three ways that the narrator's life is different from Zela's life.

   _____

   _____

   _____

   _____

3. How is your life similar to the narrator's life?

   _____

   _____

4. How is your life different from the narrator's life?

   _____

   _____

Name _____

Fiction
Compare and Contrast

Review

Read the sentence. Then write **compare** or **contrast** to tell whether the sentence compares or contrasts two things.

1. The treehouse is damp and cold like the basement.   _____

2. My dog Jeeby is much furrier and puffier than your dog Kelso.   _____

3. Cheryl's bedroom smells like flowers.   _____

4. Unlike my closet, yours is neat and organized.   _____

Answer the items.

5. Write two story elements that you can compare and contrast.

   _____

   _____

6. When you compare and contrast things in a story, can it help you to better understand the story? Explain your answer.

   _____

   _____

7. Explain how pictures can help you to compare and contrast things in a story.

   _____

   _____

   _____

Name _____

Fiction

Foreshadowing

1

Some stories have **foreshadowing**. Foreshadowing occurs when a story contains clues about what will happen later in the plot. Details that **foreshadow** can help you make predictions about the story as you read. These are examples of foreshadowing:

A character has a certain fear.

A character says or thinks that something in particular will happen or will not happen.

A character thinks or talks about luck, rewards, or punishments.

Read the paragraphs. Then answer the item.

1.   Adrian and his sister Beth waited in line to ride the Ferris wheel. They had been waiting for 20 minutes when Beth said, "I'm going to see what's taking so long."
"I hope it's not broken," Adrian called after her. Just as Beth got to the entrance to the ride, a man carrying a toolbox swung open the gate and started letting people in within minutes. Adrian and Beth were enjoying the ride. "It's a little shaky as you get higher up," Adrian said, chuckling nervously. They had a bird's-eye view of the fair. Then, all of a sudden, the ride stopped working. Their cart was stuck right at the top.

Write two details that foreshadow Adrian and Beth getting stuck at the top of the Ferris wheel.

_____

_____

_____

2.   At the fair, Ciara and Dan were in line to get an ice cream cone, when Dan saw a penny on the ground. When he reached down to pick it up, Ciara said, "I wouldn't do that. The head's facing down. That's bad luck." Dan laughed and said that having extra money is always good luck. A few minutes later, the friends were happily eating their ice cream when Dan's scoop of vanilla fell onto the pavement. "Told you!" said Ciara.

Write one detail that foreshadows what happened to Dan.

_____

_____

The Reef Thief

Keoni's class was discussing a fable about a fox who was punished for stealing bricks from an old man's house. Keoni was daydreaming, though, about swimming in the ocean. After school, he dashed home, grabbed his snorkel, and jumped into the water. Keoni lived in a house on the beach with his grandfather. Of all the things he loved about the ocean, he loved its coral reefs the most. He was amazed by the shapes and colors of the coral, as well as the fish and other strange creatures that swam around it.

Keoni discovered a small curved piece of coral. "That looks like a wave," he thought. He snapped it off and brought it home. He collected more coral the next day, and every day after that, until his grandfather realized what he was doing.

"Keoni, you mustn't take coral from the ocean!" his grandfather said.

"Why not?" Keoni asked.

His grandfather sighed. "Coral is a living thing, and it's also home to thousands of other sea creatures. How would you feel if someone came here and stole your home?"

Keoni shrugged. "I only took some small pieces, Grandfather."

"What if everyone took just some small pieces?" his grandfather asked. "Soon there would be no coral left. Don't steal any more!" Keoni's grandfather added, "You know, the ocean always takes back what belongs to it."

All that night, Keoni worried about how the ocean would take the coral back. The next day, Keoni was outside when an alarm startled him.

"That's an emergency siren!" his grandfather said. "It's a tsunami. We must go up the hill, before the giant wave hits the beach!" Keoni raced up the hill with his grandfather and all their neighbors.

An hour later, from the safety of his uncle's house, Keoni watched the tsunami crash onto the beach. The enormous wave rushed over the patio of Keoni's house, where Keoni had been looking at his coral. Keoni gasped, "Our home is flooded and destroyed!"

"Everybody's safe, though." Keoni's grandfather placed his hand on Keoni's shoulder. "That's all that matters."

As the water went back into the ocean, Keoni saw the patio furniture, along with his coral collection, get washed away. "The ocean punished me and took back what I stole," he thought. He vowed to never steal coral again.

Name _____

Fiction
Foreshadowing

2

The Reef Thief

> Some stories have **foreshadowing**. Foreshadowing occurs when a story contains clues about what will happen later in the plot. Foreshadowing can help you make predictions about what will happen later on in the story.
> These are some examples of foreshadowing:
>
> There is a conversation that teaches a character a lesson.
>
> A character says or thinks that something in particular will happen or will not happen.
>
> A character thinks or talks about luck, rewards, or punishments.

Answer the items about the story you read.

1. Explain how the fable from Keoni's class discussion foreshadows that Keoni will be punished for taking coral from the ocean.

   _____

   _____

   _____

2. Explain how the first conversation with Keoni's grandfather foreshadows what will happen to Keoni's coral collection.

   _____

   _____

   _____

3. Why does the tsunami happen, according to Keoni?

   _____

   _____

   _____

© Evan-Moor Corp. • EMC 2424 • Reading Comprehension Fundamentals

Name _____

Fiction
Foreshadowing

Review

Answer the items.

1. Explain what foreshadowing is in a story.

   _____

   _____

2. Write one example of foreshadowing that you may find in a story.

   _____

   _____

3. Do you think it's important to pay attention to foreshadowing in a story? Explain why you think so.

   _____

   _____

Read the paragraph. Then answer the question.

4.   When Melanie opened the refrigerator door, she couldn't see anything because the inside of the fridge was entirely dark. "Mom!" she called. "I think we need a new light bulb!" A few minutes later, her mom replaced the bulb, and the fridge was well lit, as usual. Later, Melanie was in her bedroom reading when the light bulb in there suddenly went out. It creeped her out because she was afraid of being in the dark. She ran out of her room and called for her dad. He replaced the light bulb in her room. Then, Melanie and her brother Jay were playing a board game with dice when one of the die rolled under the sofa. Melanie tried to switch on the flashlight to see better. She didn't want to stick her hand into a dark place. But the flashlight didn't work. "Really?" she thought. "It must need batteries." Melanie hoped that all the lights would just work how they were supposed to. That evening, a rough storm raged into Melanie's town. It made the trees sway and the streets flood. And it made the power go out at Melanie's house. She had to get used to being in the dark after all!

   How does the story foreshadow the power going out at Melanie's house?

   _____

   _____

Name _____

Fiction
Idioms

1

> An **idiom** is a phrase that has a figurative meaning that is different from its literal meaning, or what the words actually say. The literal meaning of an idiom doesn't make sense in the context of the story or paragraph it is in. For example:
>
> **Idiom:** It's raining cats and dogs.
> **Meaning:** There is a lot of heavy rainfall.
> **Sentence with Idiom:** The ground is soaked because it's raining cats and dogs.
> **Sentence Meaning:** The ground is soaked because of all the rain.
>
> You can use the context of a sentence to figure out the meaning of an idiom.

Read the sentence with the idiom. Then mark the meaning of the idiom.

1. If Mom catches you sneaking that cookie before dinner, you will **be in hot water**.
   - Ⓐ get in trouble
   - Ⓑ have to take a shower

2. I thought Becky was my friend, but now she's **giving me the cold shoulder**.
   - Ⓐ putting ice on my shoulder
   - Ⓑ ignoring me

3. I can see you're ready to go home now, but you need to **hold your horses**.
   - Ⓐ keep the horses calm
   - Ⓑ be patient and wait a little bit longer

4. I know the password to log in to the computer, but I am **drawing a blank** at the moment.
   - Ⓐ unable to remember
   - Ⓑ holding a white card

Read the sentence with the idiom. Then write the meaning of the idiom.

5. Dad told me to keep Mom's birthday party a secret, but I **let the cat out of the bag**.

_____

The Forever House

Recently my parents bought a new house. They say it's our "forever house" because they want us to live there for a long time. We haven't moved into the new house yet, though, because my parents say that it needs a lot of repairs.

My parents hired a company to do all of the repairs at the house. Last week, our entire family went to see the house. It was the first time that my brother Tony and I were seeing the house, and we were so excited.

When we got to the house, it was 7 o'clock in the evening. The crew of workers had already left for the day. Dad said that the workers probably called it a day by 6 o'clock each evening so that they wouldn't be working after dark, which wouldn't be safe.

As we stepped inside, we saw a few ladders leaned up against walls. The first room had big holes in the floor and in the wall. It looked like a fireplace was going to be built there because there were large gray stones piled up near a hole in the wall, and they looked shiny and new. Dad said, "Yes, our new home will have a fireplace." Tony and I looked at each other with huge smiles. Dad continued, "Those stones are going to surround it. They are very good quality stones, and they cost an arm and a leg."

Standing in the middle of the enormous room, I spread out my arms. "This will be my bedroom," I told Tony.

His eyes nearly popped out of his head. "What?"

I laughed. "I'm just pulling your leg."

Mom said it wasn't safe to go upstairs because there weren't any railings yet, so Tony and I stayed downstairs. As we walked around, we saw a room that looked kind of like a kitchen. It had long counters, but there was no refrigerator, stove, or microwave. "Don't worry," said Mom, laughing. "It won't be so empty when we move in."

After walking around a bit, I realized that I had a rubber ball in my pocket. Tony dared me to bounce the ball as high as the second floor balcony. I bounced the ball as hard as I could, and it just barely went higher than the second floor balcony. Tony and I laughed wildly. "See," I said, "that was a piece of cake!"

We didn't stay at the house for long. There was no electricity and no water, so we headed back to our other house in the hopes of moving to our forever house sometime soon.

Name _____

Fiction
Idioms

2

The Forever House

> When you read an **idiom**, you don't take the meaning of the words literally. Use the context of the sentence or story to figure out what the idiom means.
>
> Authors use idioms to add humor to the story.
>
> Authors also use idioms to make the narrator and characters' dialogue sound natural. Many people use idioms when they speak.

Find each bold idiom below in the story. Read the sentence it is in. Then answer the question.

1. **cost an arm and a leg**
   What do you think this idiom means? Explain why you think so.

   _____

   _____

2. **pulling your leg**
   What do you think this idiom means? Explain why you think so.

   _____

   _____

3. **piece of cake**
   What do you think this idiom means? Explain why you think so.

   _____

   _____

Answer the item.

4. Do you think the idioms in the story made the characters' conversations sound natural? Explain your answer.

   _____

   _____

© Evan-Moor Corp. • EMC 2424 • Reading Comprehension Fundamentals

149

Name _____

Fiction
Idioms

Review

Answer the items.

1. Explain what an idiom is.
   _____
   _____

2. Describe one way that you can figure out the meaning of an idiom in a story.
   _____
   _____

3. Why do you think idioms can make characters' conversations sound more natural?
   _____
   _____
   _____

Read the sentence with the idiom. Then write the meaning of the idiom.

4. Grandma always tells Salman that he is the **apple of her eye**.
   _____

5. Judy really wanted to win the singing competition, so she **sang her heart out**.
   _____

6. Pablo has to give a speech in front of the whole school, but he has **butterflies in his stomach**.
   _____

7. Whenever Mom says that she has a funny story to tell me, **I'm all ears**.
   _____

Name _____

Fiction

Historical Fiction

1

A **historical fiction** story takes place in the past.
Ask yourself these questions to see if a story is historical fiction:

Does the story have details from a certain time or place in the past?

Does the story mention things that were common in the past?

Read the paragraph. Then answer the items about what you read.

    Betsy awoke in the early hours of the morning, well before the sun had risen. She climbed out of her bed, which was made of hay, and lit a candle for light. She got ready for school by candlelight, putting on her petticoat, dress, coat, stockings, and bonnet. After getting dressed, she walked to school. Betsy was ten years old, so she was one of the oldest children at the schoolhouse. That meant that she always had to help Mistress Toro, the teacher, with the other children. All of the children in town attended the schoolhouse, which had one classroom for all of the children, ages 5 to 12. When the children in town turned 13, they usually began working as helpers. Some children helped the miller, who made flour out of wheat. Some of the children helped Mistress Toro at the school. Betsy wished that she could work with her father, the blacksmith, who used hot fire all day to melt metal. He made all of the town's metal objects, such as swords, knives, and shovels. But Betsy knew that no girl had ever worked as a blacksmith in her town, so she would probably be a teacher, like Mistress Toro.

1. What details tell you that this is historical fiction?

_____

_____

_____

2. Write one clothing item that Betsy wears that was common in the past.

_____

Circle the things that you would **not** find in a story with a setting in the 1800s.

3. roller coaster   book   castle   light switch

   cellphone   feather pen   computer   mirror

Traveling to Oregon

We have been moving westward, slowly but steadily, in our family's covered wagon for two months now, and we're still not even in Oregon yet. It is now November, and the air is getting colder. The road has been hard for me, my ma, my pa, my brother Eli, my sister Goody, our oxen, and our horse. Our journey isn't nearly over, but we are at a standstill for now in Wyoming.

Life on the road is difficult. There are no signs on the road telling us the right way to go. We have taken a wrong turn a time or two, which has really set us back. And we go for days without seeing other travelers on the trail.

We eat stale bread dipped in water for most of our meals. We still have a little bit of salted meat that Ma made back in September, before we got on the wagon trail. The salted meat has lasted for months, as it's supposed to, but it is very tough and hurts my gums every time I bite into it. But so does the bread.

Luckily, we are starting to come into some hills as we move farther west. For a long time on the trail, when we were crossing over the flat plains of the country, we had the hot sun beating down on us and our animals, and it was hard to find streams to get water from. But the hilly terrain of Wyoming has offered streams with cold mountain water, and that has brought us some comfort. We've also been seeing more trees. Ma says that she'll make us some pine needle tea because Eli has a bad cough. She'll make it once Pa makes a fire. She said that she may even make a soup out of the tree bark and leaves that we see on the trail, because food is so scarce right now.

We are stopped on the trail for a few days because one of our wagon wheels has broken. Pa and Eli are trying to repair it. In the meantime, Pa says that it may do us good to have a rest. Pa has seen some coyotes, and he says that he may be able to get some fur that we can make into vests or blankets, as the weather is getting cooler.

We all have work to do, even though we're traveling. Since we left our home in Virginia, Goody and I have had to mend our dresses two times already. It's much harder than you think to sew while you're in a bumpy wagon that's shaking on an uneven trail. We all, including the tired animals, look forward to getting to Oregon and starting a new life.

Name _____

Fiction

Historical Fiction

2

Traveling to Oregon

> A **historical fiction** story takes place in the past. Even though the story may seem true, it is not true. These things are common in historical fiction:
>
> The story mentions objects that people had or used in the past.
>
> The story is about things that can really happen in the real world.
>
> The story gives details about things people did in the past.

Answer the questions about the story you read.

1. What details tell you that this story is historical fiction?

   _____

   _____

   _____

2. How is traveling different for the narrator's family than it is for you today?

   _____

   _____

   _____

3. Could all of the things that happen in the story be possible in the real world? Explain why you think so.

   _____

   _____

4. What part of the story do you think would be most difficult for you to deal with? Explain why you think so.

   _____

   _____

© Evan-Moor Corp. • EMC 2424 • Reading Comprehension Fundamentals

Fiction

Historical Fiction

Review

Name _____

Answer the items.

1. Write one way that you can tell a story is historical fiction.

   _____

   _____

2. Explain how a historical fiction story is different from other kinds of stories.

   _____

   _____

   _____

   _____

Write **true** or **false** for the sentence.

3. In a historical fiction story, a family could fly on a spaceship to take a vacation on the moon. _____

4. In a historical fiction story, a group of pioneers can decide to start their own town near a swamp. _____

Read the pair of sentences. Then tell if it describes a historical fiction. Explain why or why not.

5. Abraham stepped onto the ship that would carry him to Europe. It was the fastest way for him to get there to visit his grandparents.

   _____

   _____

6. To write her letter, Henrietta dipped the feather into ink, then she quickly formed the letters on the paper before the ink dried. This was a lot of work, so it took her three hours to write a one-page letter.

   _____

   _____

Name _____

Fiction

Realistic Fiction

1

A **realistic fiction** story is about things that can really happen. Even though the events and settings seem real, the story is not true. These are important things to remember about realistic fiction:

The events usually take place in the present time.

The setting is real or seems like a place where people really live.

The story is about things that can really happen.

Read the pair of sentences. Circle the pair if it describes a realistic fiction.

1. Zaria went to the space center in Florida. She learned about the first moon landing, which happened in 1969.

2. Dylan met a friendly alien. The alien went to school with Dylan.

3. Lynsey went to Jupiter in a flying car. She stayed in a Jupiter colony for two weeks.

4. Owen read a story about space exploration. He hopes that humans will have the technology to travel to Mars in the future.

5. An astronaut came to Max's class. Max missed it, though, because he was home sick.

Read the paragraph. Then tell if it describes a realistic fiction. Explain why you think so.

6.   Suki's science teacher is an owl. He is the only teacher at her school that is not a human. At first, Suki thought it would be weird to learn science from an owl, but it's actually not that different from having an ordinary human as a teacher.

_____
_____

7.   Hondo is making a model of Venus for a science project. He is using construction paper, marbles, and paint to create it. He is putting a lot of effort into the project.

_____
_____

Mother's Helper

"Hurry up, Priya!" Mom said. "You can't be late for your first day of work! And here's my cellphone, in case you need to use it to call me."

Priya's neighbor, Mrs. Collins, was planning a fundraiser and needed someone to keep her four-year-old son, Terrell, busy for a couple of hours.

"It's not babysitting," her mother had said, "because Mrs. Collins will be there. You'll be a mother's helper."

Priya was excited to see what it would be like to be in charge. In the past, she had babysitters who would watch her when her parents went out for an evening, but she had never watched younger children herself.

Two hours later, at Mrs. Collins' house, Priya was no longer wondering what it was like to be in charge. She was trying to stop Terrell from throwing shoes and toys across his playroom. And when she finally got him to stop doing that, Terrell grabbed the cellphone that her mother had given her and started pressing all the keys. "Hey, that's my mom's phone!" exclaimed Priya.

She got the phone out of Terrell's hands just as he started chasing the cat around the room. She put the phone to her ear to make sure Terrell didn't call anyone by mistake. "Hello?" she said, as she grabbed Terrell's shirt to stop him from chasing the cat. No answer.

Then Priya got an idea. "Who wants a snack?" she asked.

"I do!" screamed Terrell.

Priya went into the kitchen, where Mrs. Collins was talking on the phone. Her laptop was open on the kitchen counter, and papers lay everywhere.

Priya took some strawberries back down to the playroom, and a minute later, Terrell threw a fit because they weren't all the same size. Priya sighed. Being a mother's helper was a lot of work! Just then, Mrs. Collins came downstairs and asked Priya if she'd like to stay an extra hour.

"I still have a lot to do," Mrs. Collins said. "I talked to your mom, and she said it's fine for you to stay until four, if you'd like to." Priya bit her lip. She really wanted to go back home and rest, but she could tell that Mrs. Collins needed the extra help, so she agreed to stay.

For the last hour with Terrell, Priya put on a movie for them to watch, and Terrell actually fell asleep. When she finally got back home, she was exhausted. "Hmm, I'm not sure if I want to be in charge ever again," she thought.

Name _____

Fiction
Realistic Fiction
2

Mother's Helper

> A **realistic fiction** story is about things that can really happen. The setting is usually in the present and in a place that could be real. These are important things to remember about realistic fiction:
>
> The events usually take place in the present time.
>
> The characters have problems that real people deal with.
>
> The story is about things that are possible in the real world.

Answer the items about the story you read.

1. What details tell you that this story takes place in the present time?

   _____

   _____

2. Describe any problems that Priya has in the story.

   _____

   _____

   _____

3. Could all of the things that happen in the story be possible in the real world? Explain why you think so.

   _____

   _____

   _____

4. Is it realistic that Priya would feel tired after her experience? Explain why you think so.

   _____

   _____

© Evan-Moor Corp. • EMC 2424 • Reading Comprehension Fundamentals

Name _____

Fiction
Realistic Fiction

Review

Answer the items.

1. Write one way that you can tell a story is realistic fiction.

   _____
   _____

2. Explain how a realistic fiction story is different from other kinds of stories.

   _____
   _____
   _____
   _____

Write **true** or **false** for the sentence.

3. In a realistic fiction story, a family could adopt a dog from an animal shelter and give it a safe home.   _____

4. In a realistic fiction story, a family could adopt a baby dragon and teach it how to speak English.   _____

Read the paragraph. Then tell if it describes a realistic fiction. Explain why or why not.

5.   Bernardo's dad took the whole family to a basketball game last weekend. Bernardo got a hot dog, a fruit smoothie, and a new basketball jersey. He had so much fun.

   _____
   _____
   _____

6.   Dennis wanted to know how it feels to be a centipede. He made a wish, and an elf appeared. The elf said that he'd turn Dennis into a centipede for one day only.

   _____
   _____

Name _____

Fiction
Mystery

1

> A **mystery** is a story about characters trying to solve a puzzling problem. Sometimes, characters try to discover the cause of a puzzling event. A mystery always has clues that help the characters figure out the answer. These are examples of things that can happen in a mystery:
>
> A character's item is lost, missing, or damaged.
>
> A character wants to learn another character's secret.
>
> A character wants to find out who is responsible for something that happened.

Read the paragraph. Then answer the items.

Emma came home from school to find one of her tomato plants knocked over. "Who did this?" she wondered. She looked down and noticed a candy wrapper lying on the patio. It was a wrapper for a cherry lollipop. She knew that her neighbor, Tommy, had just gotten a big bag of cherry lollipops. As Emma took a closer look, she saw muddy shoe prints on the patio. "Whoever did this hopped over the fence and landed in the mud when they came into our yard," she thought. Emma knew this because there was mud all around the fence that circled her yard. She walked the perimeter of the entire yard, looking for any patches of wet mud. She found one patch of wet mud near the part of the fence that was shared by her yard and Tommy's.

1. Who probably knocked over the tomato plant in Emma's yard? Explain how clues in the story helped you form your opinion.

   _____

   _____

   _____

   _____

2. In this mystery, Emma is trying to _____.
   - Ⓐ find out what caused the mud patch to be wet
   - Ⓑ learn another character's secret
   - Ⓒ find something that is missing or stolen
   - Ⓓ find out who is responsible for something that happened

© Evan-Moor Corp. • EMC 2424 • Reading Comprehension Fundamentals

The Top-Secret Mission

On Friday morning, Agent Herring arrived at Detective Headquarters at precisely the same time as her detective partner, Agent Klue.

"Morning, Klue," she said. "Any interest in going bowling this weekend?"

"Can't," Agent Klue said. "I'm going on a mission for the entire weekend."

"Ooh, exciting," Agent Herring said. "Where are you going?"

"Can't say," Klue said. "Top secret."

Agent Herring was immediately seized by curiosity. "What is he doing this weekend?" she wondered. She decided to keep an eye on him for clues.

That morning, Agent Klue appeared to be busy. He jotted down notes, sent emails, and made phone calls. When Agent Herring walked over to Agent Klue's desk to deliver some documents, he was shopping for binoculars online.

"Why are you purchasing binoculars?" she asked.

"Can't say," Klue said. "Top secret."

"I know," Herring thought. "I'll use my camera to take some close-up pictures of his desk and the notes he's been jotting down all morning."

Agent Herring grabbed her camera and tiptoed around the corner, where Klue couldn't see her. Just then, Agent Klue's phone rang. "Hello," he said quietly. "Oh, it's you." Klue spoke very quietly and scribbled some notes. "Perfect," he said. "When the eagle lands, let me know." He hung up.

Around the corner, Agent Herring had heard only part of his conversation. "Hmm," she thought. "What does Klue mean when he says *when the eagle lands*? At least I took some photos with my camera. Those should give me a clue."

At the end of the day, Agent Herring and Agent Klue stepped into the elevator together. Agent Klue held a stack of papers, including a map that he had printed out earlier. Agent Herring could only see the corner of the map, but that was enough. She smiled and said, "Have fun bird watching, Klue."

Agent Klue looked shocked. "How did you figure out my secret?" he asked.

"Easy," Agent Herring said. "You were shopping for new binoculars, something people use for bird watching. You were also drawing doodles of birds. I saw evidence of that in the photos I took of your desk. But what really tipped me off was that map you're holding. It shows the Stony River, which passes under some gigantic cliffs. I just happen to know that there's a bald eagle nest on one of those cliffs. Your eagle comment makes sense now. The eagle has landed, Klue."

"Well done, Herring," said Klue. "See you on Monday."

Name _____

Fiction
Mystery

2

The Top-Secret Mission

> A **mystery** is a story about characters trying to solve a puzzling problem. Sometimes, characters try to learn a secret or answer a puzzling question.
>
> A mystery is like a puzzle because a character puts all the clues together, like puzzle pieces, to figure out the answer.

Answer the items about the story you read.

1. Explain what Agent Herring is trying to figure out or learn in the story.

   _____

   _____

2. Write one thing Agent Herring does to get clues.

   _____

   _____

3. What makes Agent Herring so curious?

   _____

   _____

4. Explain how Agent Herring uses the clues in the story to figure out what she is trying to learn.

   _____

   _____

5. Were you surprised by the ending of the story? Explain why or why not.

   _____

   _____

© Evan-Moor Corp. • EMC 2424 • Reading Comprehension Fundamentals

Name _____

Fiction
Mystery

Review

Answer the items.

1. Mark the sentence that tells something that is common in mysteries.
   Ⓐ A character wants to find out who is responsible for something that happened.
   Ⓑ A character travels to other planets or into the future.
   Ⓒ The author tells the important differences and similarities between two characters.
   Ⓓ The setting is long ago, and the characters are people who lived in the past.

2. Explain what a mystery is in your own words.
   Explain why clues are important in a mystery.

   _____
   _____
   _____

Read the paragraphs. Then answer the question.

3.   "Where is my lunchbox?" Ferris wondered. When he looked in the cupboard where his lunchbox was supposed to be, he didn't see it. He looked inside the dishwasher, and, even though he didn't see the lunchbox, he did see the thermos he'd used at lunch the day before. "So, I must have taken my lunchbox out of my backpack when I got home from school yesterday," he thought. Suddenly, Ferris noticed a big can of bug spray on the counter. The warning label said that the spray should not come in contact with food or any containers that hold food. "Hmm, Mom must have used the bug spray after I went to bed last night," he thought.

       Then, Ferris saw a note stuck on the fridge from his mom. The note said, "Ferris, I went to work early this morning. Your lunch is packed in a brown paper bag in the fridge. We'll get you a new lunchbox after school today."

   What do you think happened to Ferris's lunchbox? Explain how you used the clues to form your opinion.

   _____
   _____
   _____

Answer Key

 These answers will vary. Examples are given.

Page 7

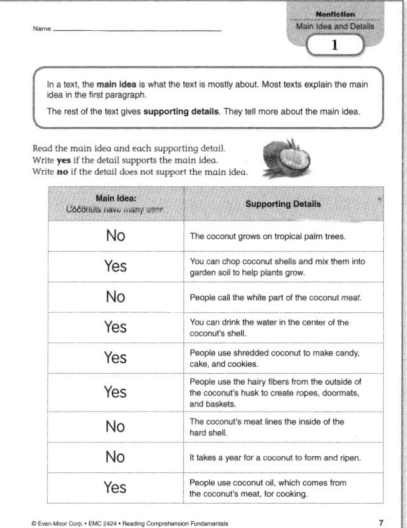

Page 8

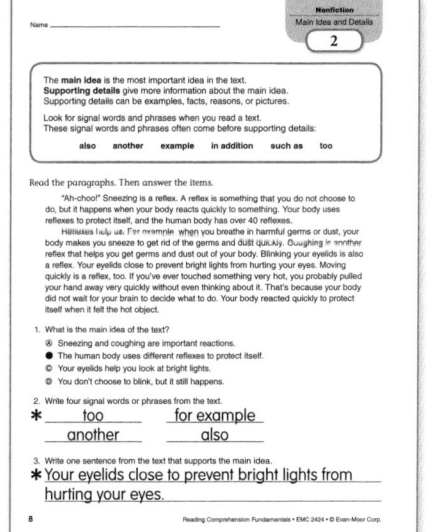

Page 10

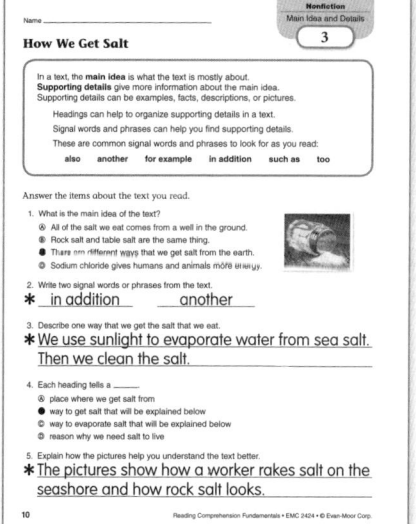

Page 11

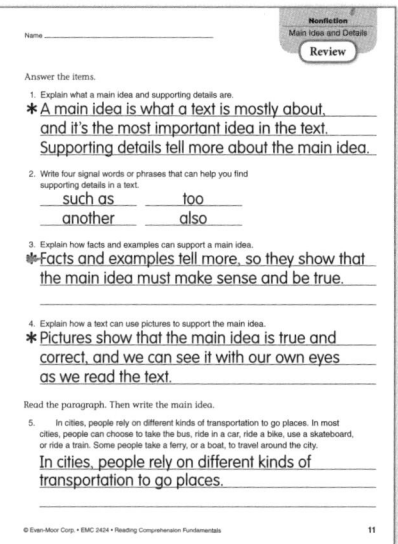

Page 12

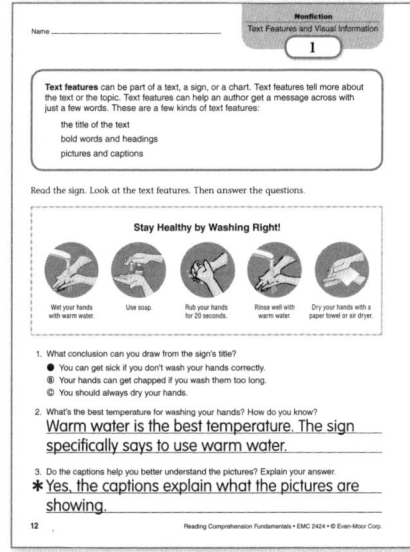

Page 13

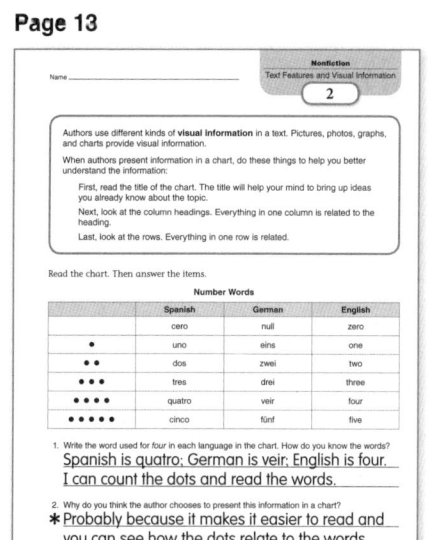

Page 15

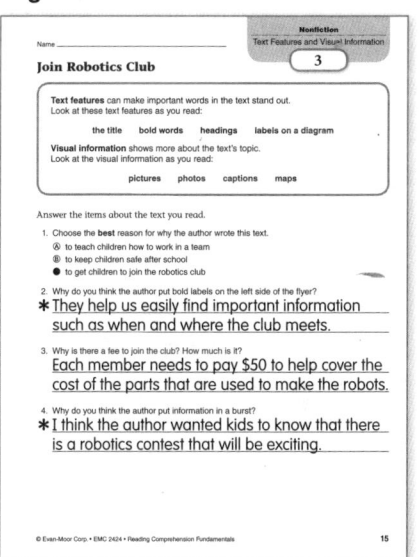

Page 16

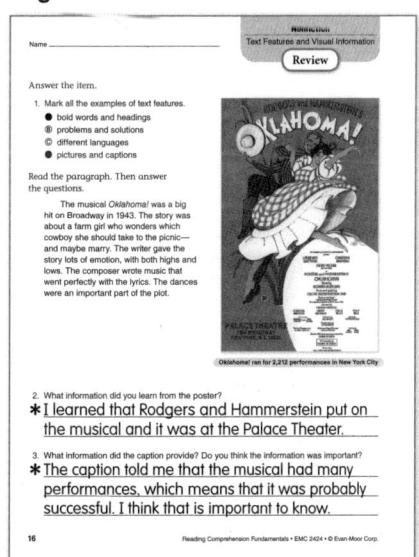

Page 17

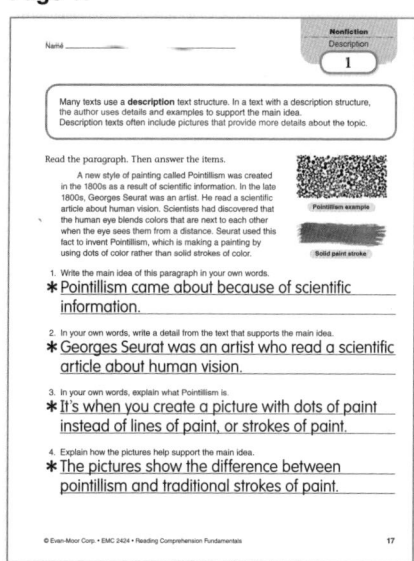

✱ These answers will vary. Examples are given.

Page 19
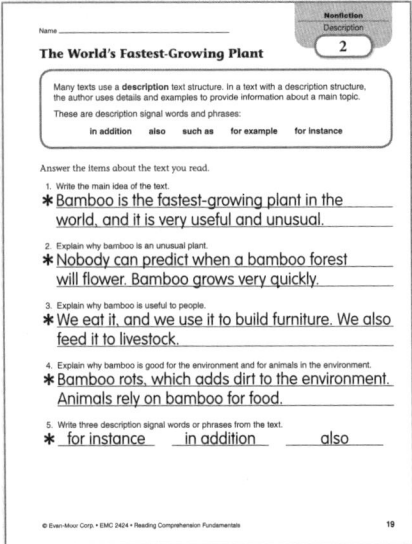

Page 20

Page 21
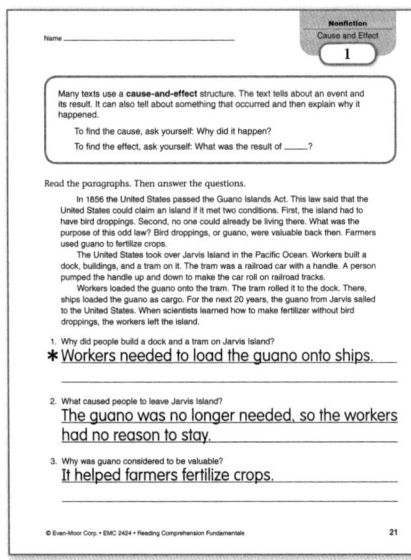

Page 22
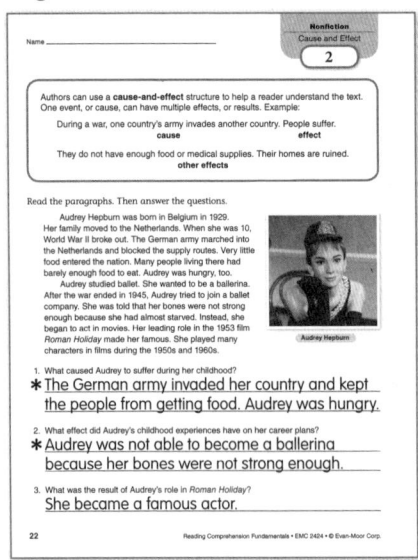

Page 24
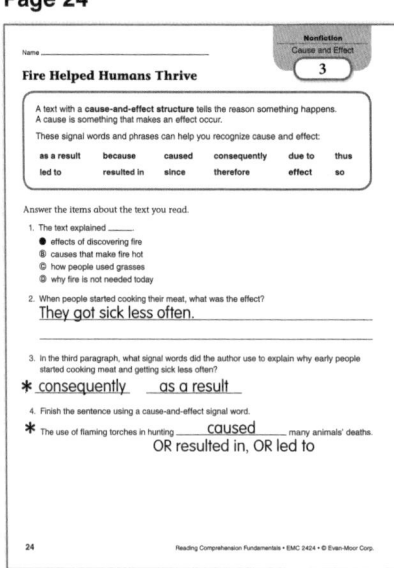

Page 25
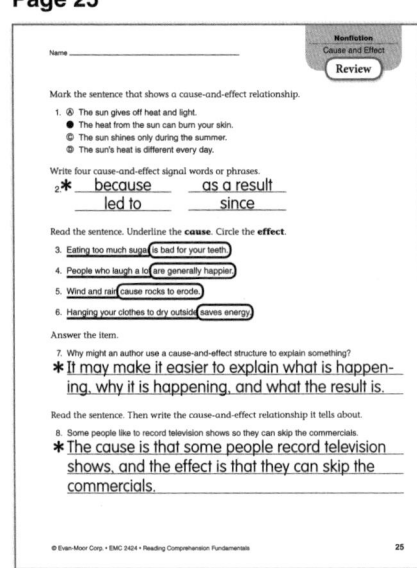

Page 26
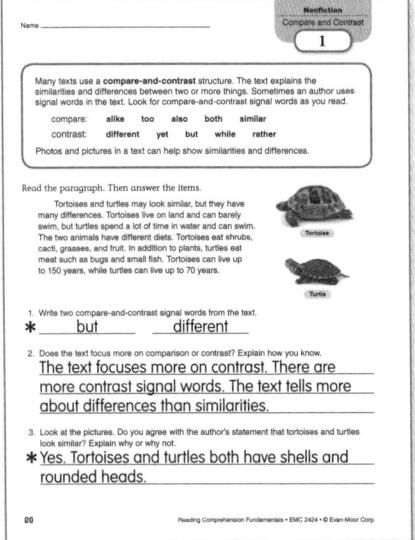

Page 27
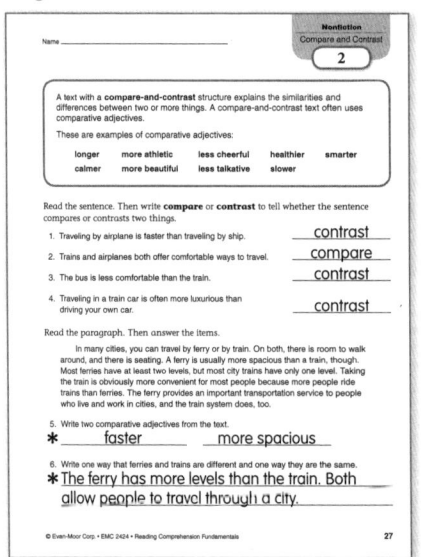

Page 29
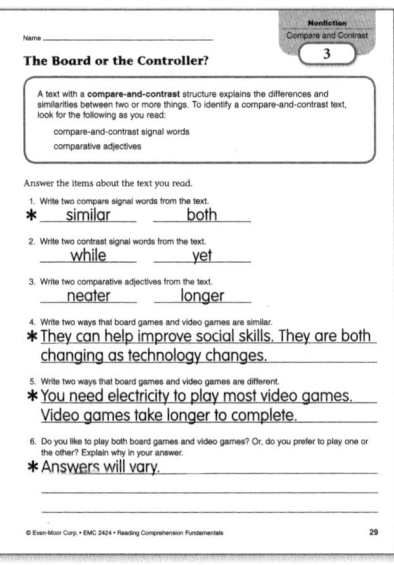

These answers will vary. Examples are given.

Page 30
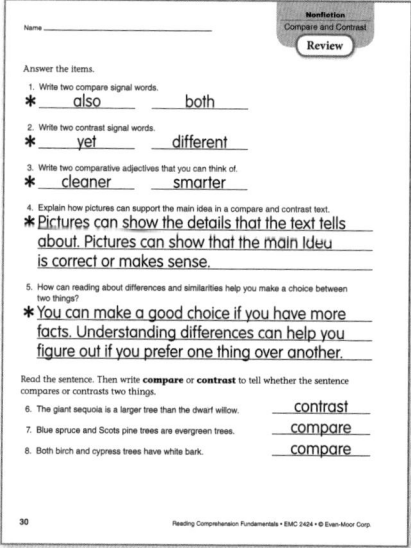

Page 31
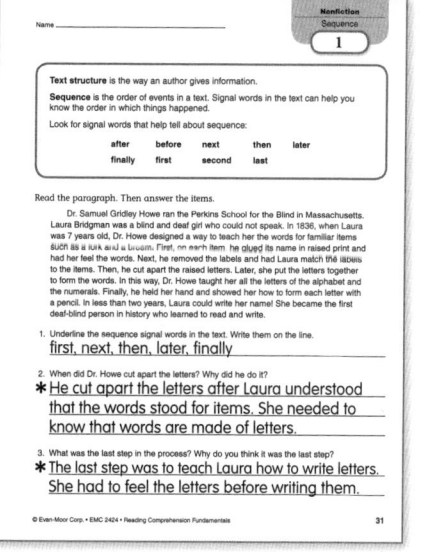

Page 33
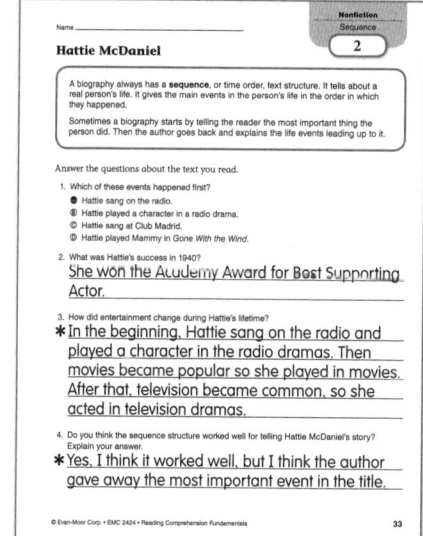

Page 34
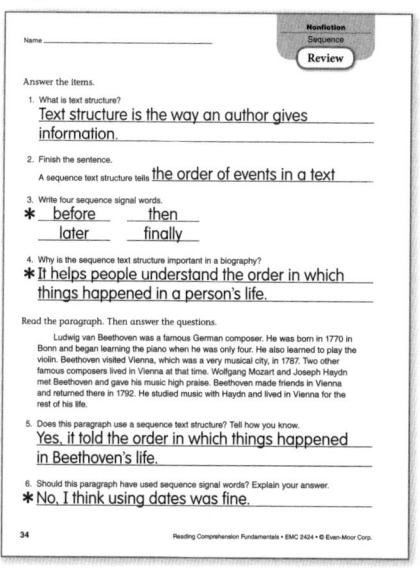

Page 35
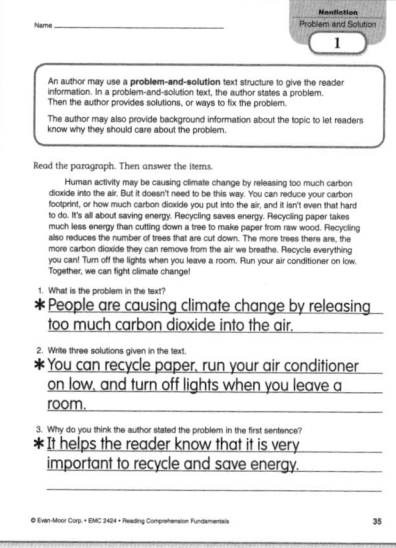

Page 36
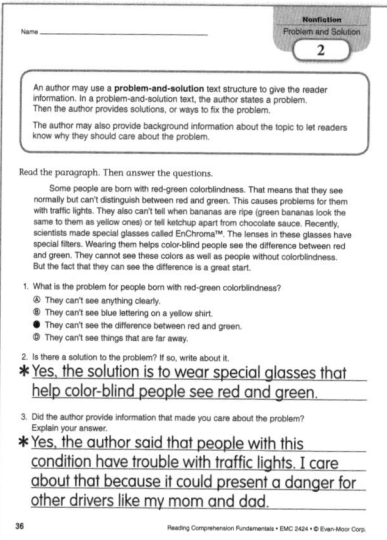

Page 38
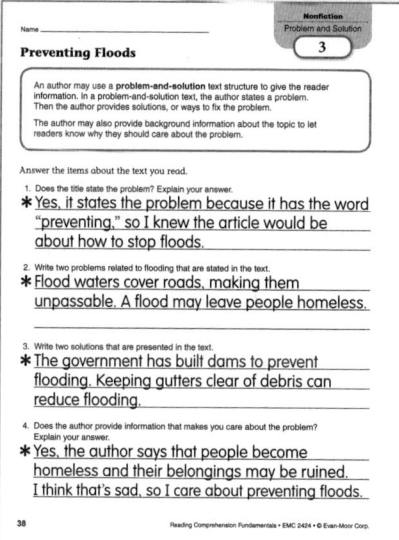

Page 39
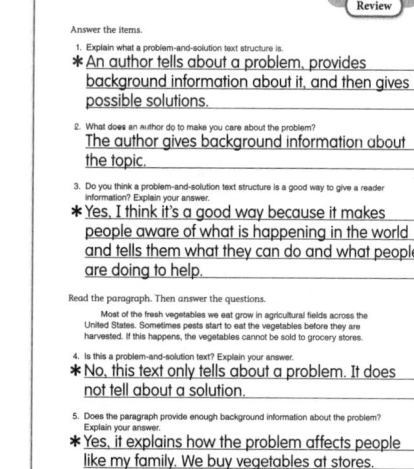

Page 40
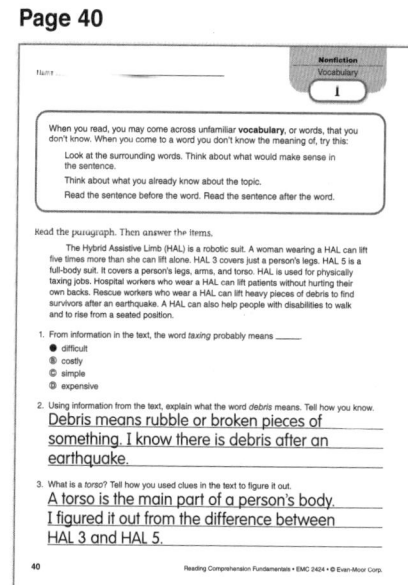

These answers will vary. Examples are given.

Page 41
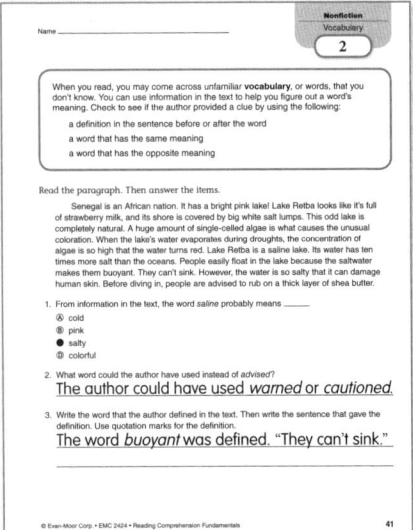

Page 43
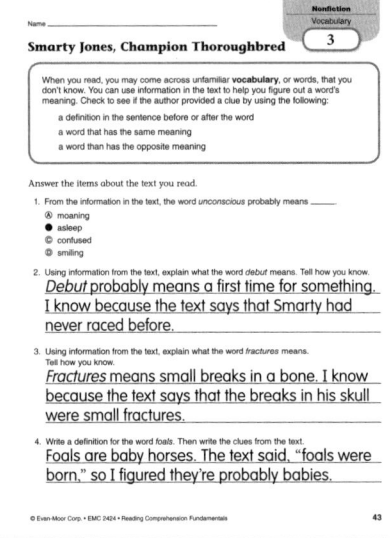

Page 44
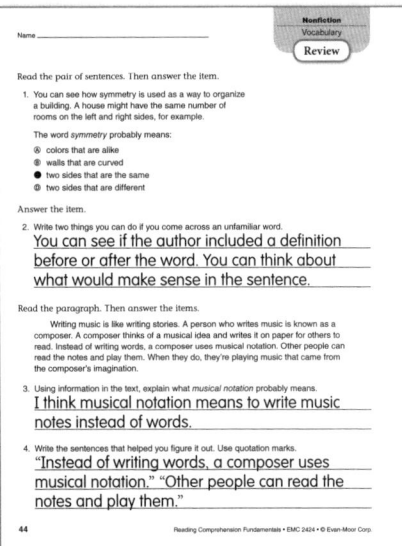

Page 45
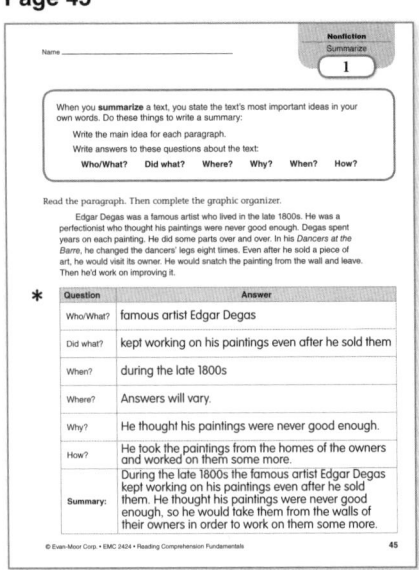

Page 46
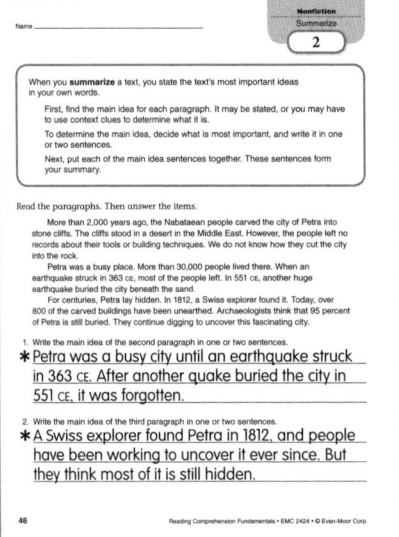

Page 48
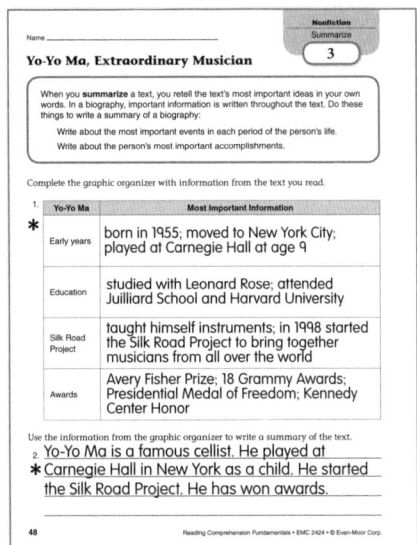

Page 49
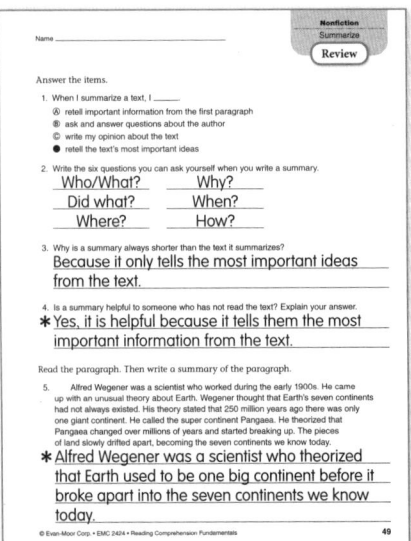

Page 50
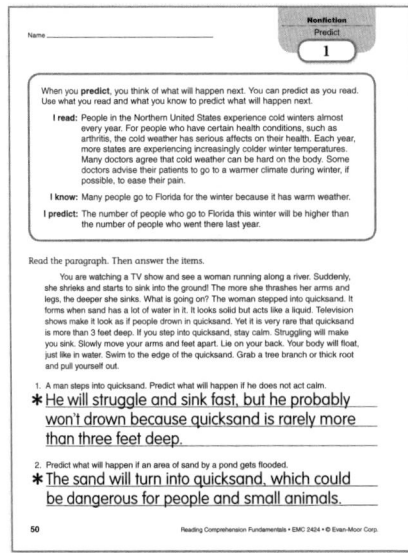

Page 51
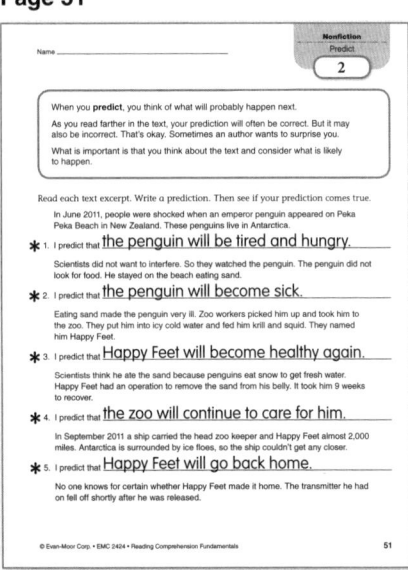

These answers will vary. Examples are given.

Page 53
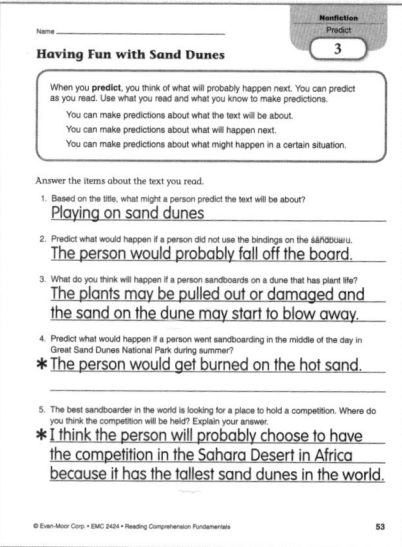

Page 54

Page 55
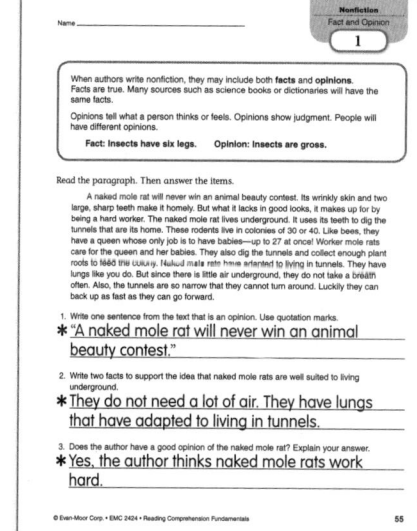

Page 56
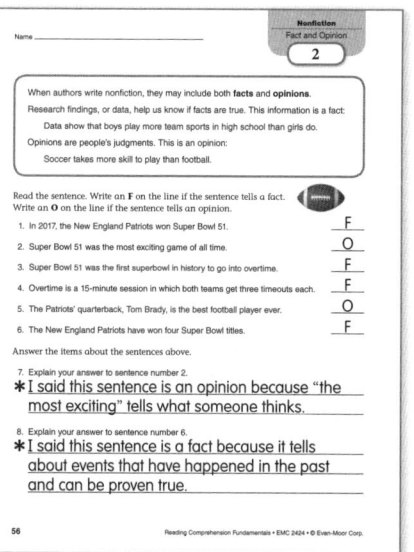

Page 58
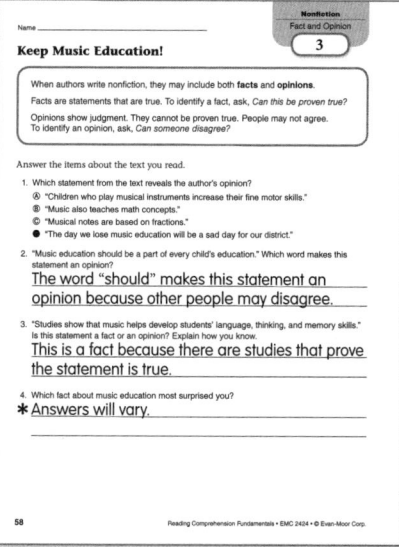

Page 59
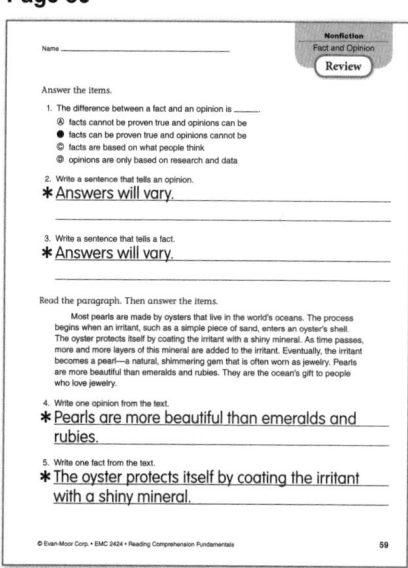

Page 60
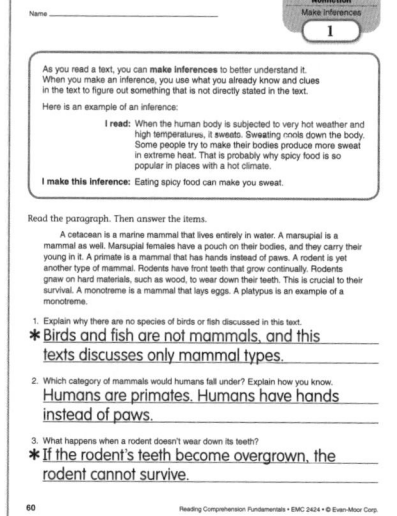

Page 61
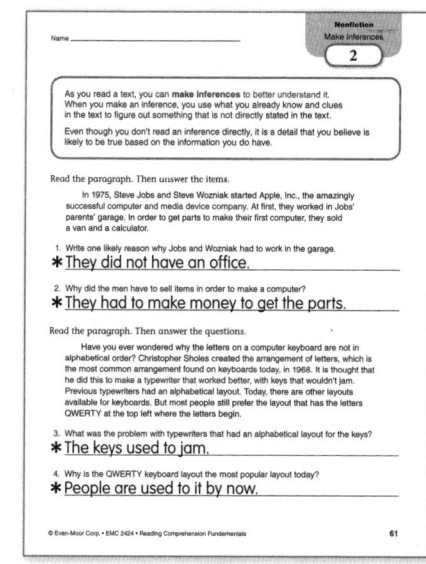

Page 63
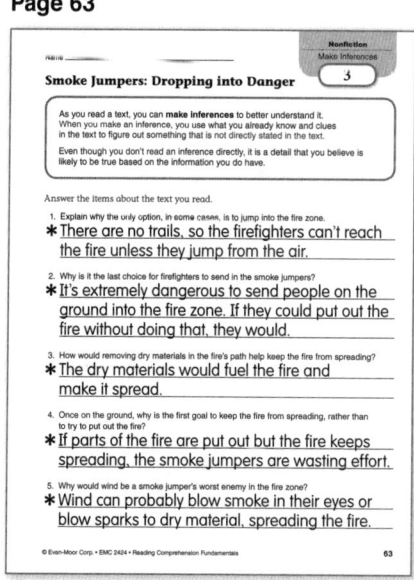

These answers will vary. Examples are given.

Page 64
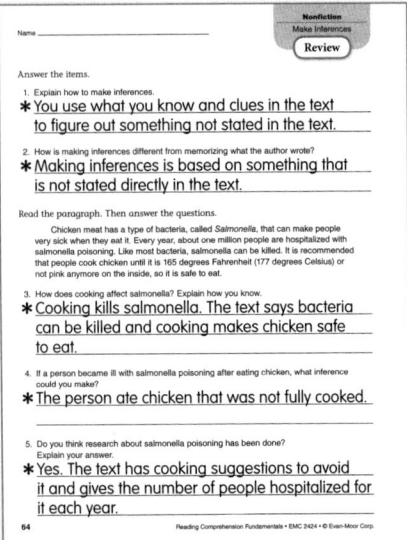

Page 65
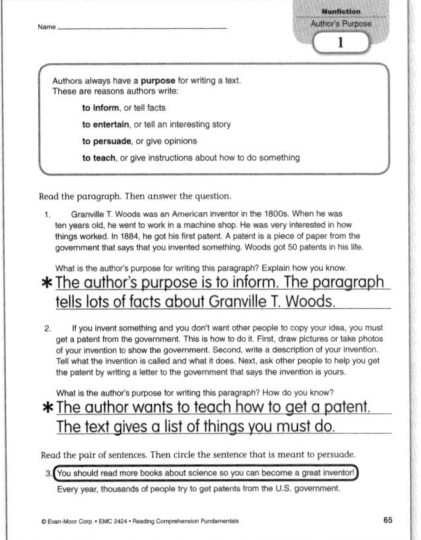

Page 66
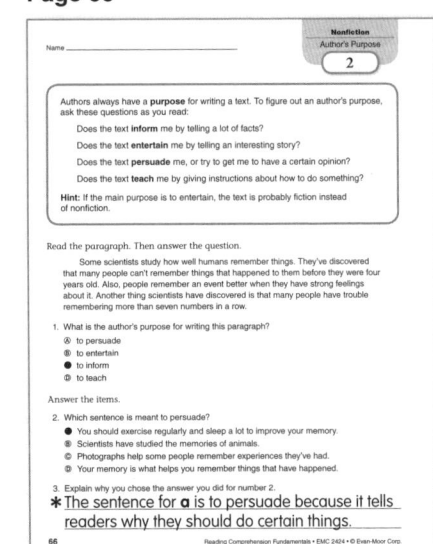

Page 68
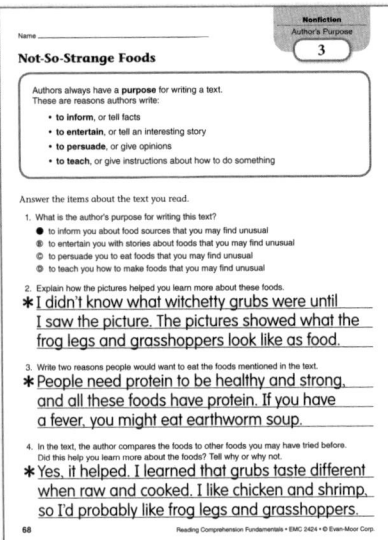

Page 69
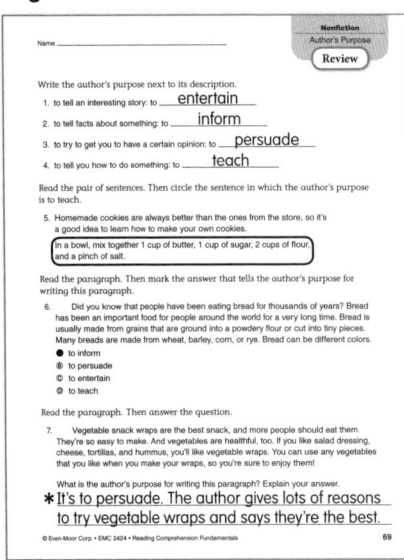

Page 70
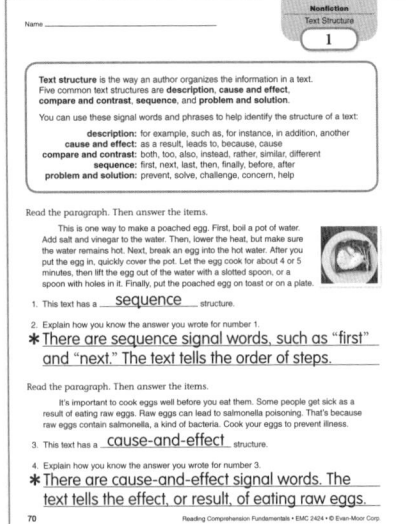

Page 72
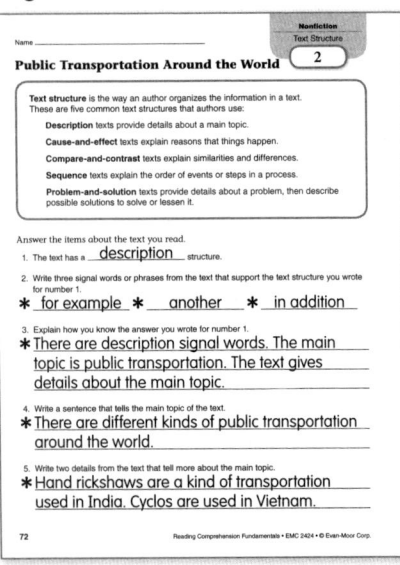

Page 73
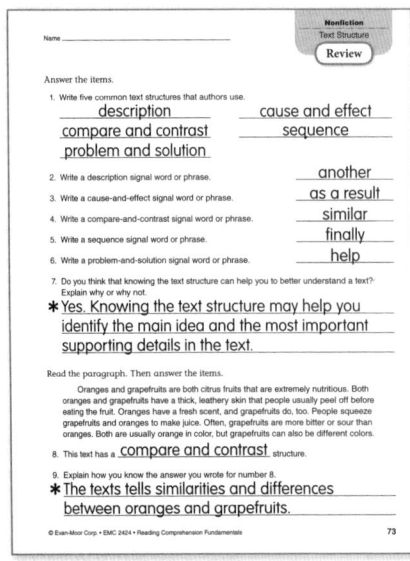

Page 74
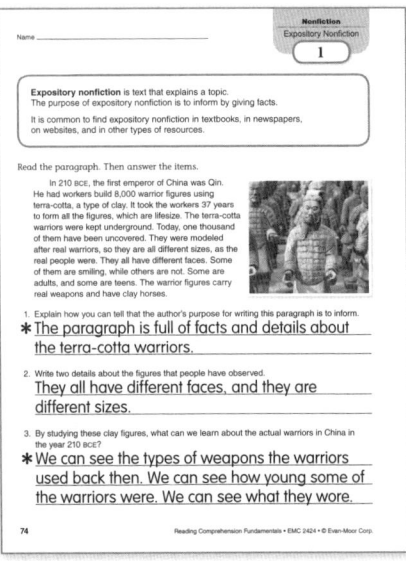

These answers will vary. Examples are given.

Page 76

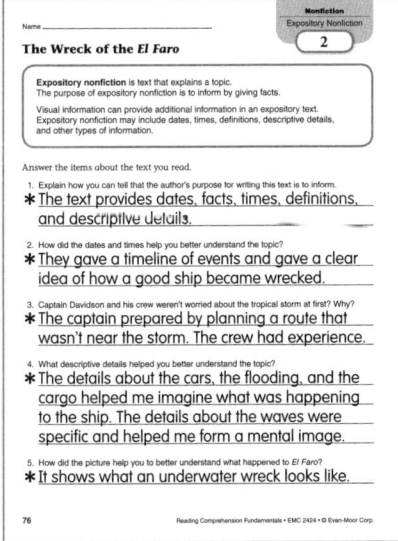

1. Explain how you can tell that the author's purpose for writing this text is to inform.
* The text provides dates, facts, times, definitions, and descriptive details.

2. How did the dates and times help you better understand the topic?
* They gave a timeline of events and gave a clear idea of how a good ship became wrecked.

3. Captain Davidson and his crew weren't worried about the tropical storm at first? Why?
* The captain prepared by planning a route that wasn't near the storm. The crew had experience.

4. What descriptive details helped you better understand the topic?
* The details about the cars, the flooding, and the cargo helped me imagine what was happening to the ship. The details about the waves were specific and helped me form a mental image.

5. How did the picture help you to better understand what happened to El Faro?
* It shows what an underwater wreck looks like.

Page 77

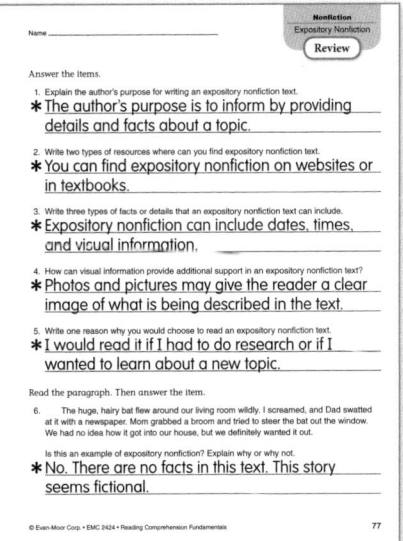

1. Explain the author's purpose for writing an expository nonfiction text.
* The author's purpose is to inform by providing details and facts about a topic.

2. Write two types of resources where you can find expository nonfiction text.
* You can find expository nonfiction on websites or in textbooks.

3. Write three types of facts or details that an expository nonfiction text can include.
* Expository nonfiction can include dates, times, and visual information.

4. How can visual information provide additional support in an expository nonfiction text?
* Photos and pictures may give the reader a clear image of what is being described in the text.

5. Write one reason why you would choose to read an expository nonfiction text.
* I would read it if I had to do research or if I wanted to learn about a new topic.

6. [paragraph question]
Is this an example of expository nonfiction? Explain why or why not.
* No. There are no facts in this text. This story seems fictional.

Page 78

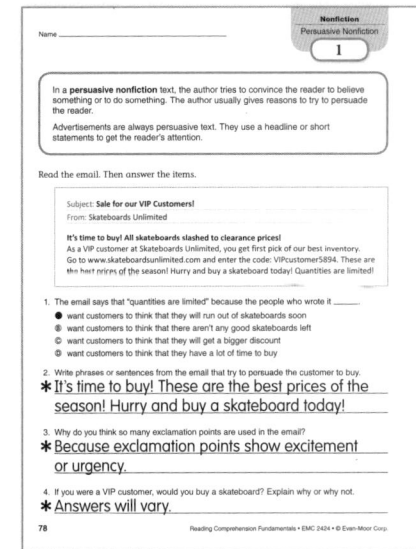

1. The email says that "quantities are limited" because the people who wrote it ___.
● want customers to think that they will run out of skateboards soon
○ want customers to think that there aren't any good skateboards left
○ want customers to think that they will get a bigger discount
○ want customers to think that they have a lot of time to buy

2. Write phrases or sentences from the email that try to persuade the customer to buy.
* It's time to buy! These are the best prices of the season! Hurry and buy a skateboard today!

3. Why do you think so many exclamation points are used in the email?
* Because exclamation points show excitement or urgency.

4. If you were a VIP customer, would you buy a skateboard? Explain why or why not.
* Answers will vary.

Page 80

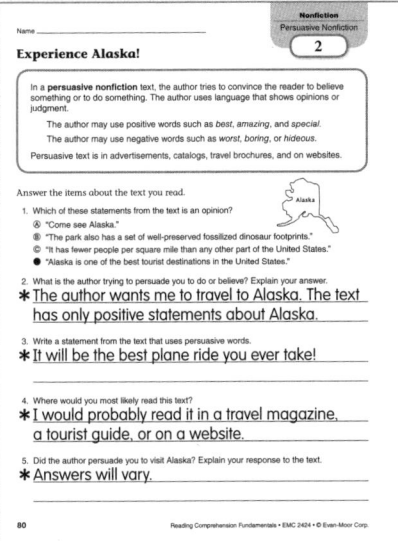

1. Which of these statements from the text is an opinion?
○ "Come see Alaska."
● "The park also has a set of well-preserved fossilized dinosaur footprints."
○ "It has fewer people per square mile than any other part of the United States."
○ "Alaska is one of the best tourist destinations in the United States."

2. What is the author trying to persuade you to do or believe? Explain your answer.
* The author wants me to travel to Alaska. The text has only positive statements about Alaska.

3. Write a statement from the text that uses persuasive words.
* It will be the best plane ride you ever take!

4. Where would you most likely read this text?
* I would probably read it in a travel magazine, a tourist guide, or on a website.

5. Did the author persuade you to visit Alaska? Explain your response to the text.
* Answers will vary.

Page 81

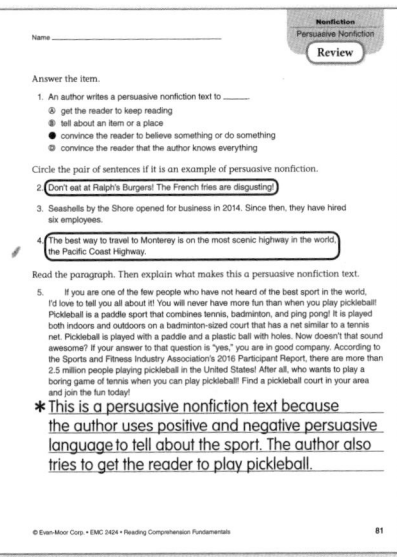

1. An author writes a persuasive nonfiction text to —
○ get the reader to keep reading
○ tell about an item or a place
● convince the reader to believe something or do something
○ convince the reader that the author knows everything

Circle the pair of sentences if it is an example of persuasive nonfiction.
2. [circled] Don't eat at Ralph's Burgers! The French fries are disgusting!
3. Seashells by the Shore opened for business in 2014. Since then, they have hired six employees.
4. [circled] The best way to travel to Monterey is on the most scenic highway in the world, the Pacific Coast Highway.

Read the paragraph. Then explain what makes this a persuasive nonfiction text.
5. [paragraph]
* This is a persuasive nonfiction text because the author uses positive and negative persuasive language to tell about the sport. The author also tries to get the reader to play pickleball.

Page 82

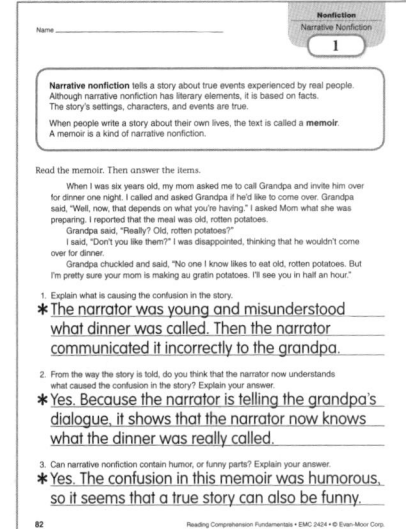

1. Explain what is causing the confusion in the story.
* The narrator was young and misunderstood what dinner was called. Then the narrator communicated it incorrectly to the grandpa.

2. From the way the story is told, do you think that the narrator now understands what caused the confusion in the story? Explain your answer.
* Yes. Because the narrator is telling the grandpa's dialogue, it shows that the narrator now knows what the dinner was really called.

3. Can narrative nonfiction contain humor, or funny parts? Explain your answer.
* Yes. The confusion in this memoir is humorous, so it seems that a true story can also be funny.

Page 84

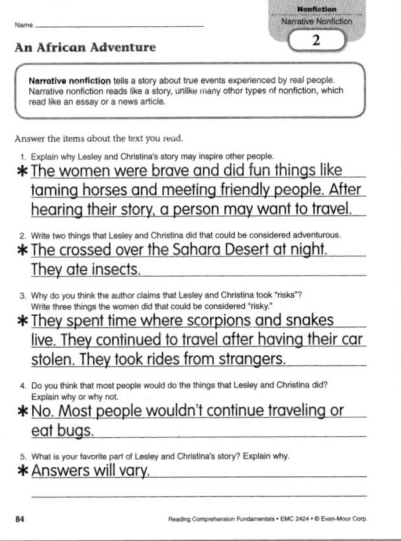

1. Explain why Lesley and Christina's story may inspire other people.
* The women were brave and did fun things like taming horses and meeting friendly people. After hearing their story, a person may want to travel.

2. Write two things that Lesley and Christina did that could be considered adventurous.
* The crossed over the Sahara Desert at night. They ate insects.

3. Why do you think the author claims that Lesley and Christina took "risks"? Write three things the women did that could be considered risky.
* They spent time where scorpions and snakes live. They continued to travel after having their car stolen. They took rides from strangers.

4. Do you think that most people would do the things that Lesley and Christina did? Explain why or why not.
* No. Most people wouldn't continue traveling or eat bugs.

5. What is your favorite part of Lesley and Christina's story? Explain why.
* Answers will vary.

Page 85

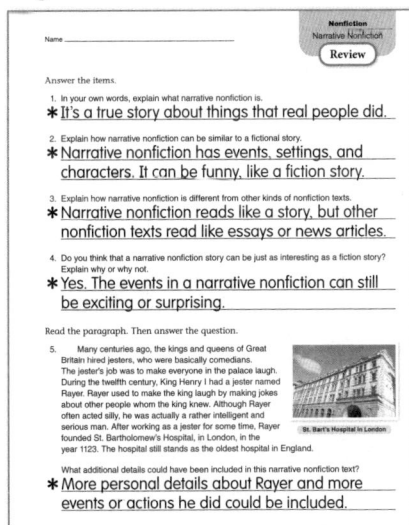

1. In your own words, explain what narrative nonfiction is.
* It's a true story about things that real people did.

2. Explain how narrative nonfiction can be similar to a fictional story.
* Narrative nonfiction has scenes, settings, and characters. It can be funny, like a fiction story.

3. Explain how narrative nonfiction is different from other kinds of nonfiction texts.
* Narrative nonfiction reads like a story, but other nonfiction texts read like essays or news articles.

4. Do you think that a narrative nonfiction story can be just as interesting as a fiction story? Explain why or why not.
* Yes. The events in a narrative nonfiction can still be exciting or surprising.

Read the paragraph. Then answer the question.
5. [paragraph]
What additional details could have been included in this narrative nonfiction text?
* More personal details about Rayer and more events or actions he did could be included.

Page 86

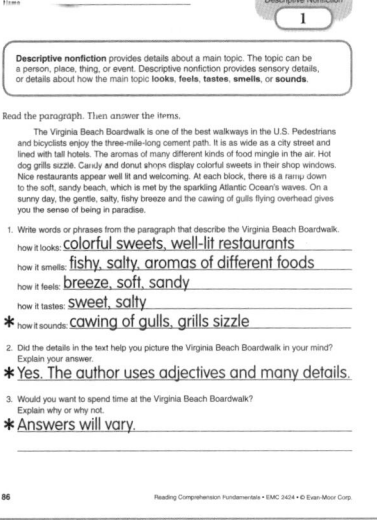

1. Write words or phrases from the paragraph that describe the people who visit the Virginia Beach Boardwalk.
how it looks: colorful sweets, well-lit restaurants
how it smells: fishy, salty, aromas of different foods
how it feels: breeze, soft, sandy
how it tastes: sweet, salty
* how it sounds: cawing of gulls, grills sizzle

2. Did the details in the text help you picture the Virginia Beach Boardwalk in your mind? Explain your answer.
* Yes. The author uses adjectives and many details.

3. Would you want to spend time at the Virginia Beach Boardwalk? Explain why or why not.
* Answers will vary.

These answers will vary. Examples are given.

Page 88
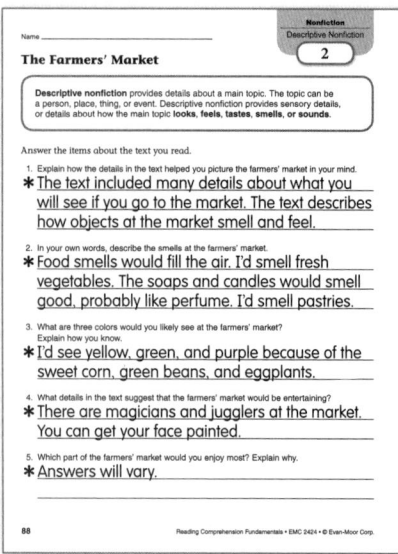

Page 89
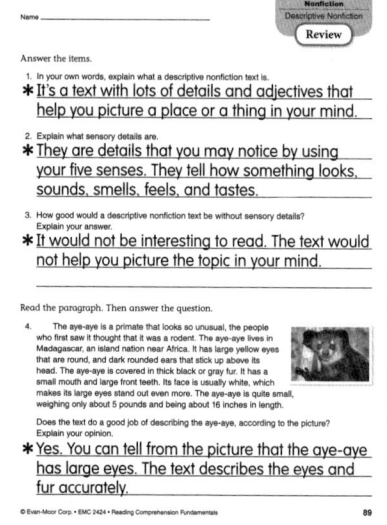

Page 90
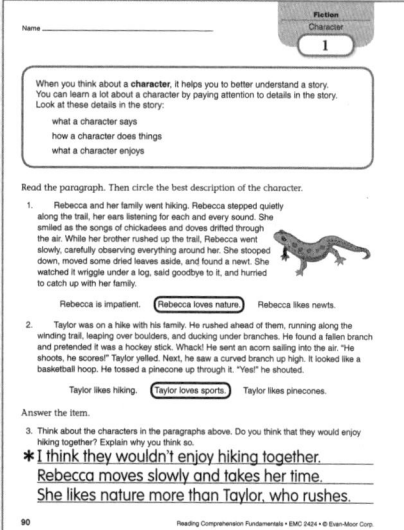

Page 91
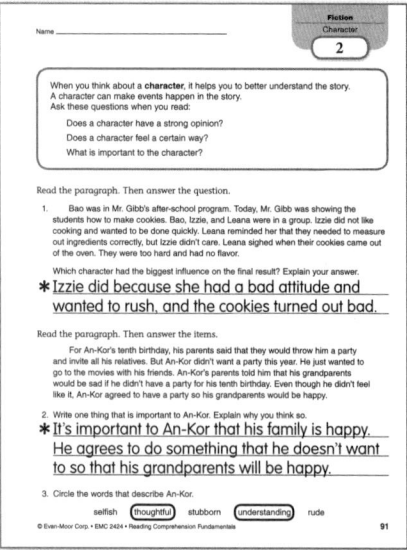

Page 93
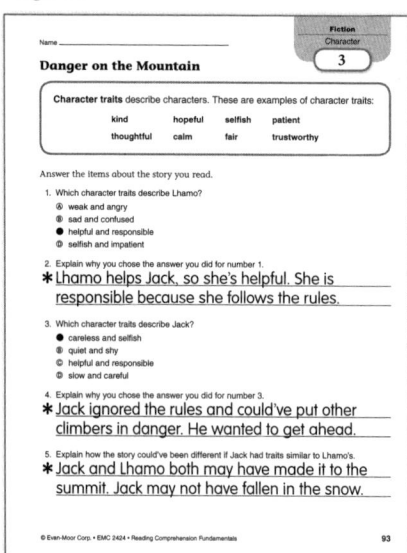

Page 94
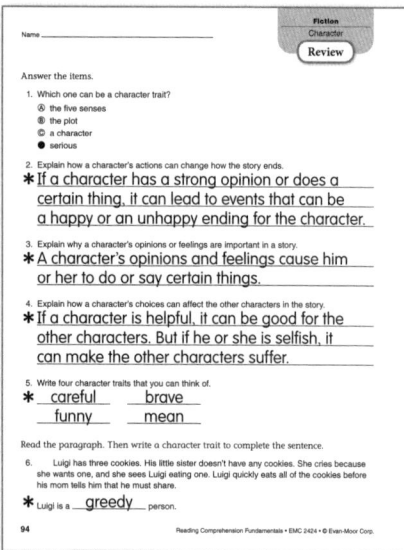

Page 95
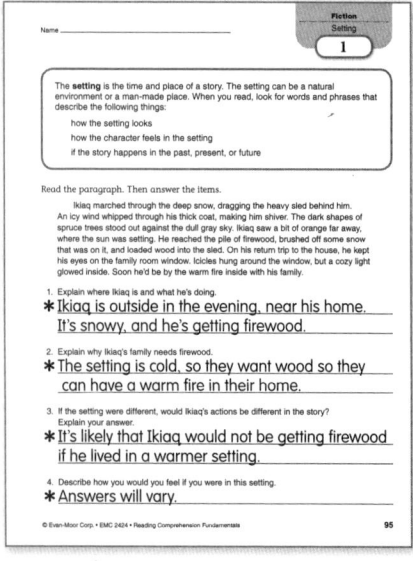

Page 96
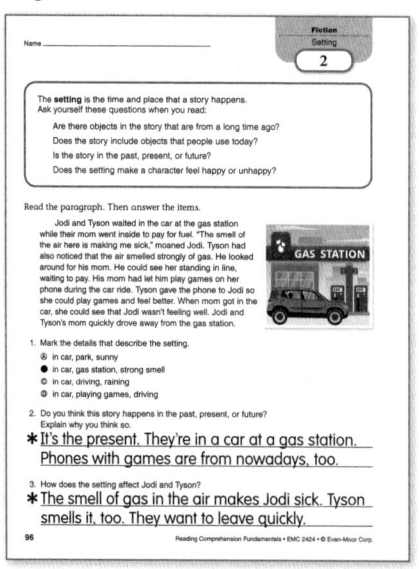

Page 98
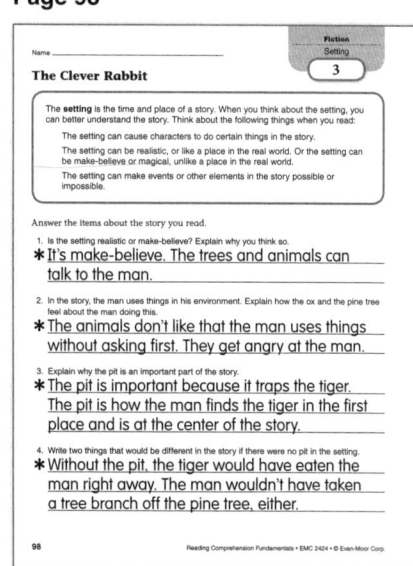

✱ These answers will vary. Examples are given.

Page 99
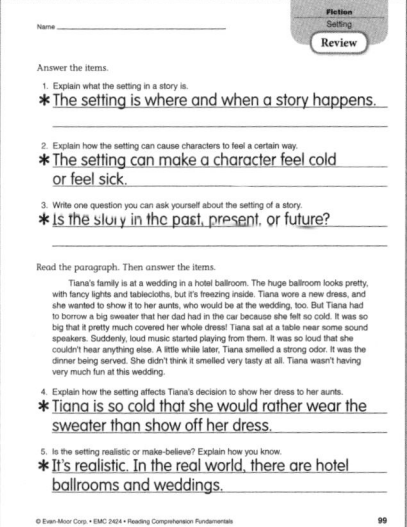

Page 100
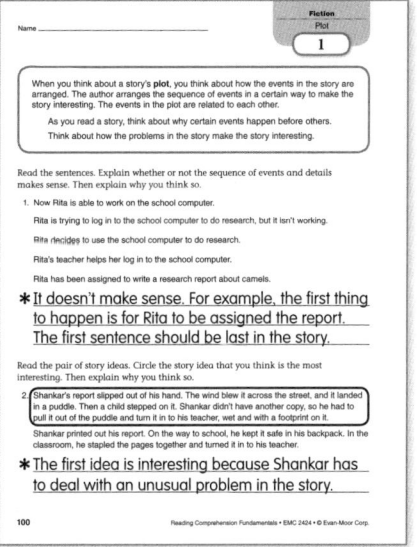

Page 101
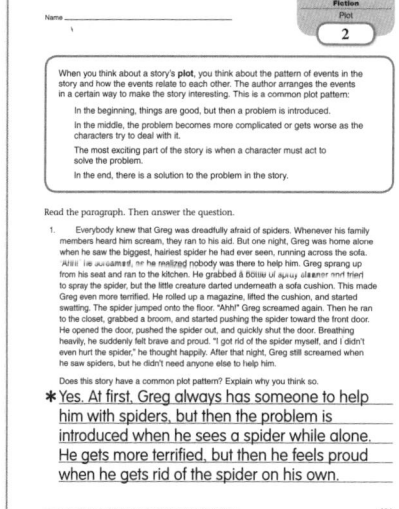

Page 103
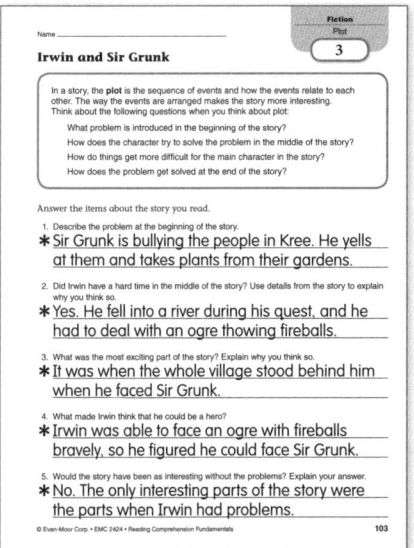

Page 104
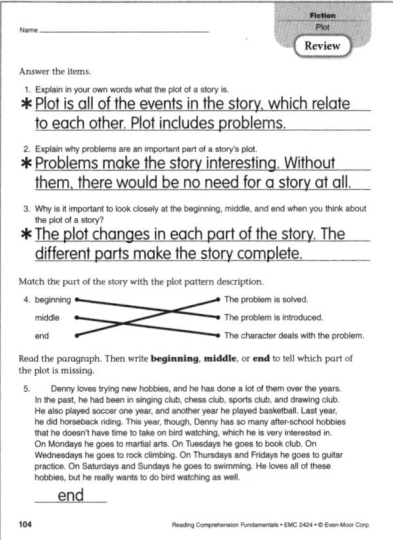

Page 105
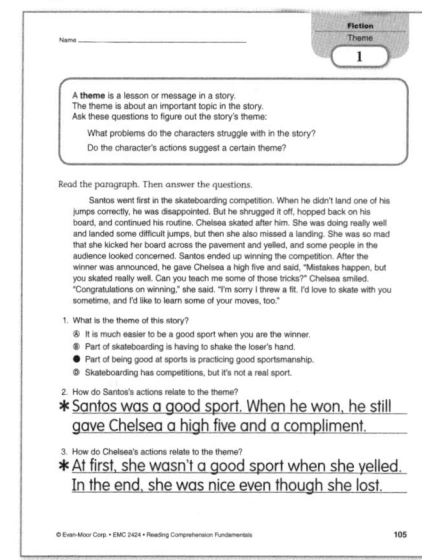

Page 106
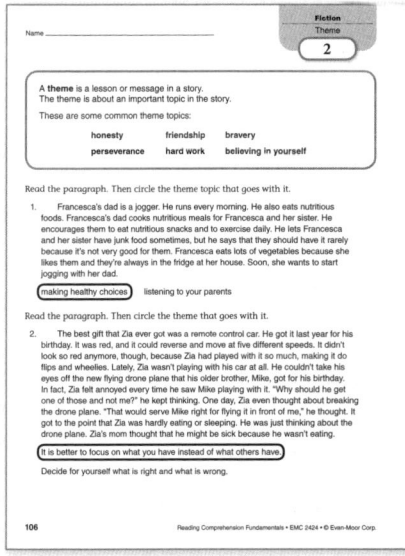

Page 108
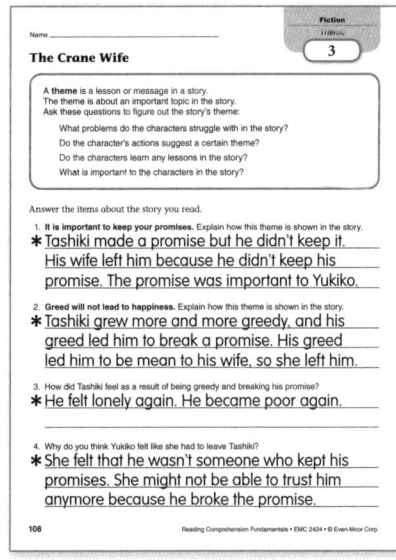

Page 109
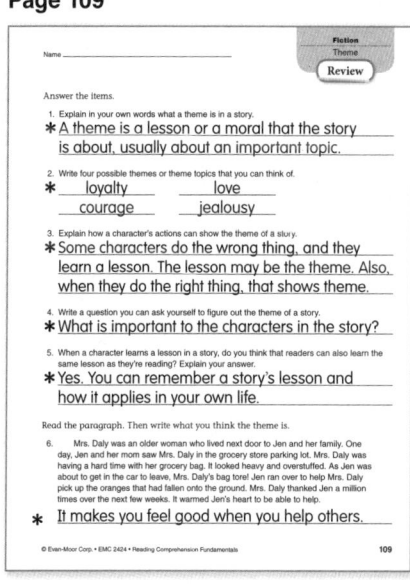

☀ These answers will vary. Examples are given.

Page 110
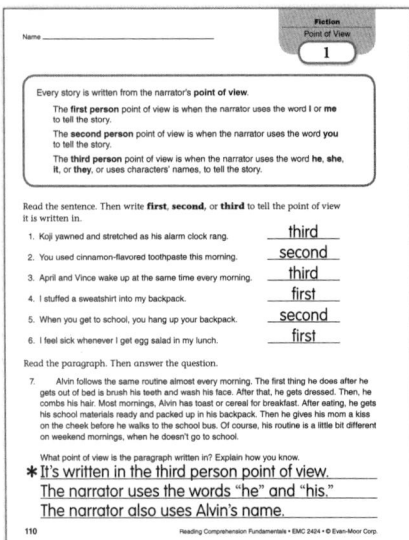

Page 111
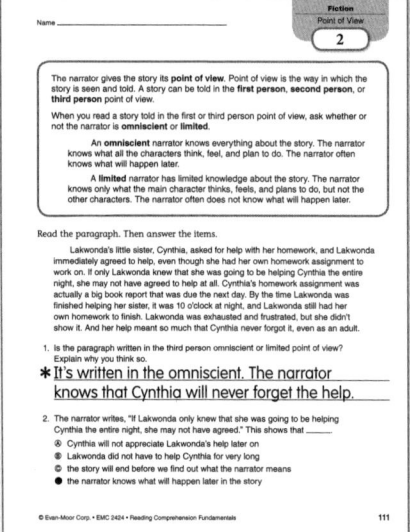

Page 113
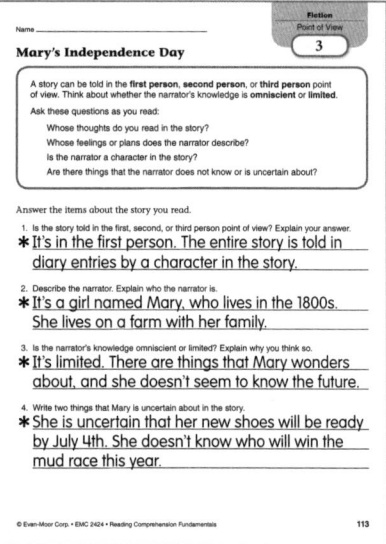

Page 114
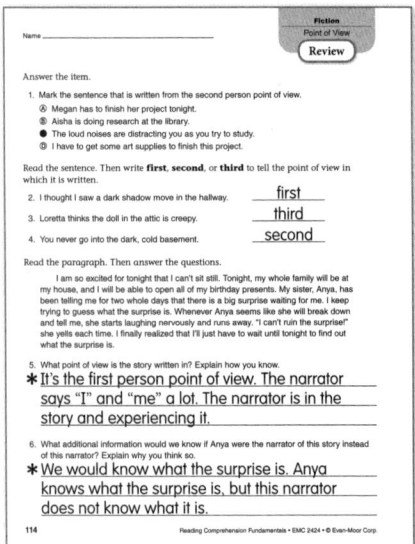

Page 115
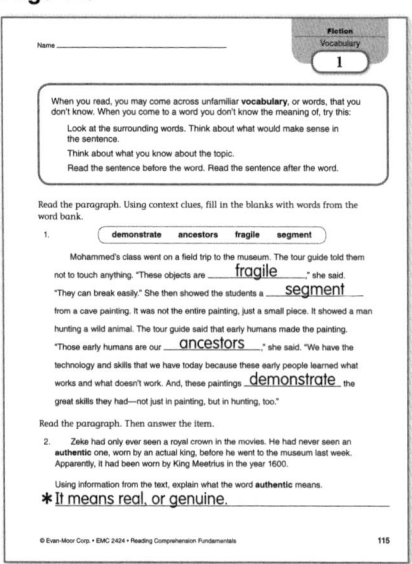

Page 117
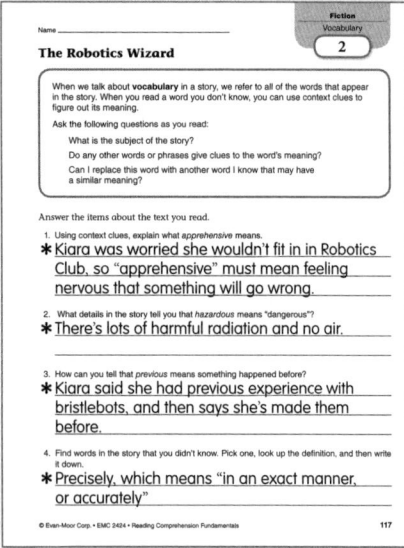

Page 118
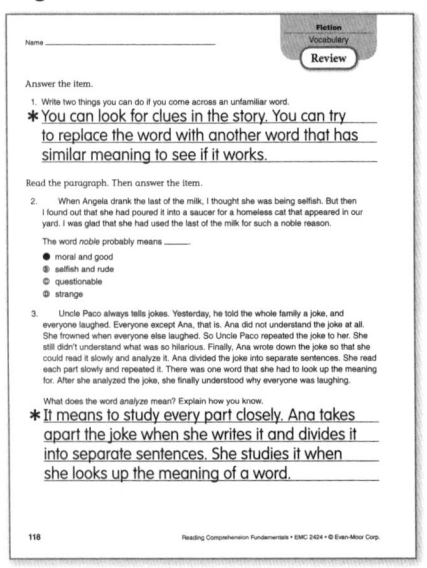

Page 119

Page 121
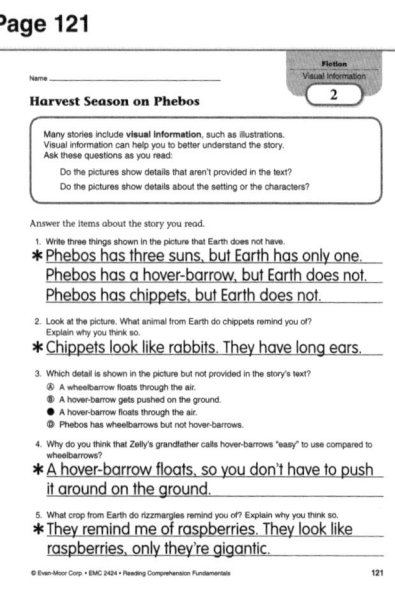

* These answers will vary. Examples are given.

Page 122
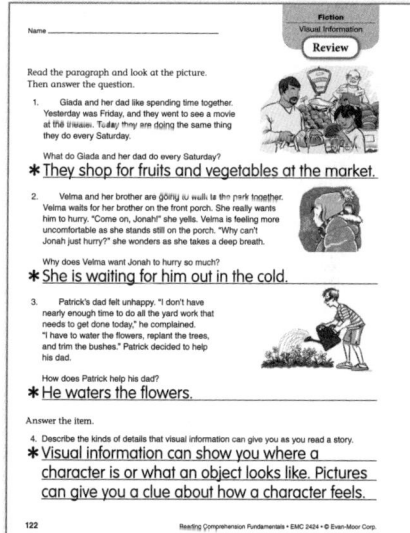

Page 123
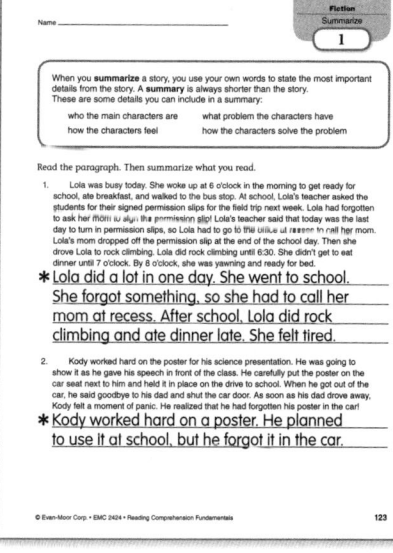

Page 125
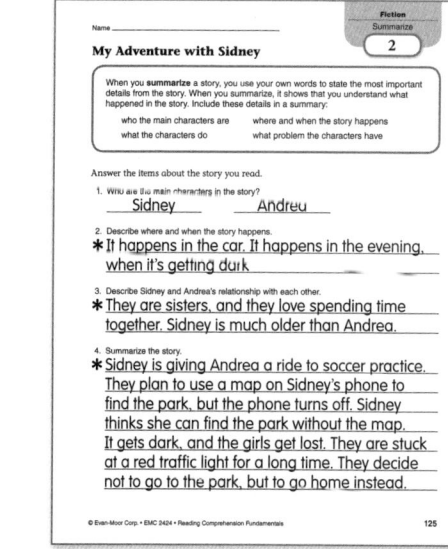

Page 126
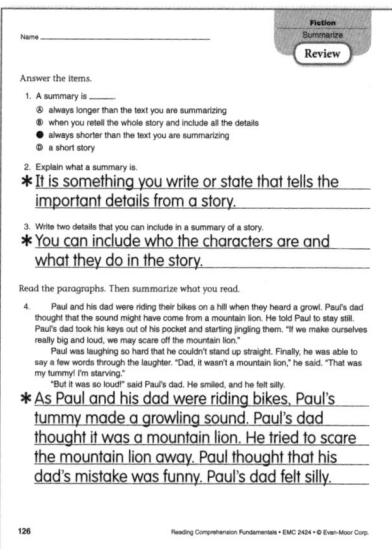

Page 127
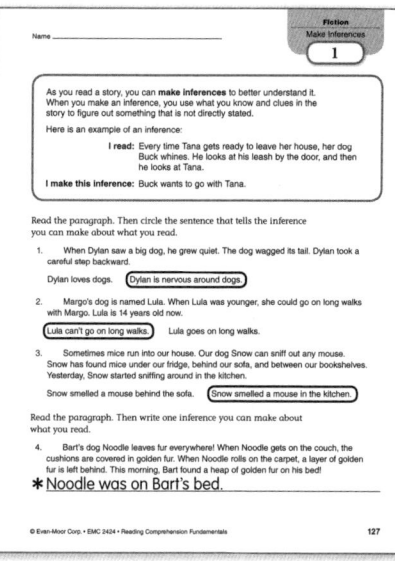

Page 129
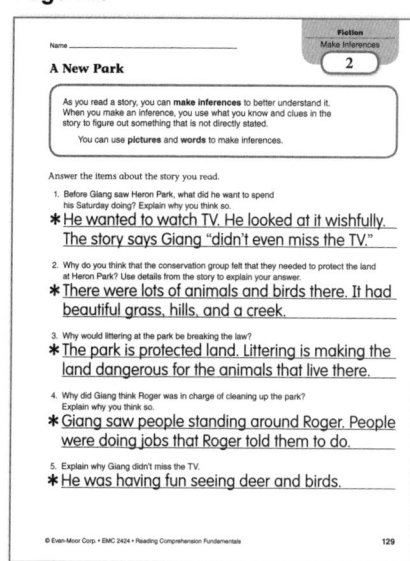

Page 130
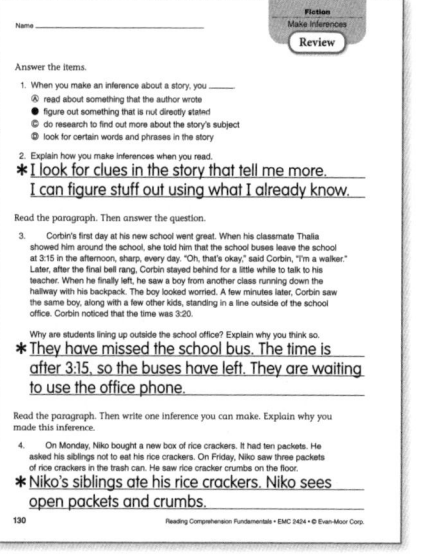

Page 131
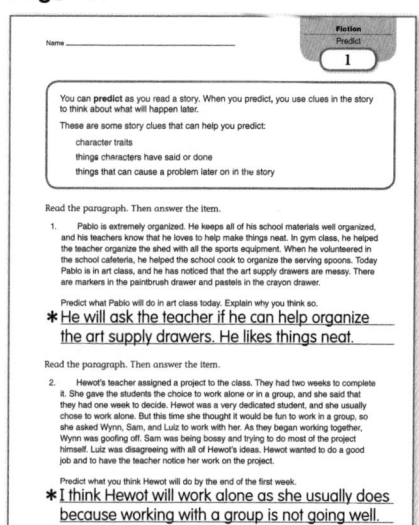

Page 133
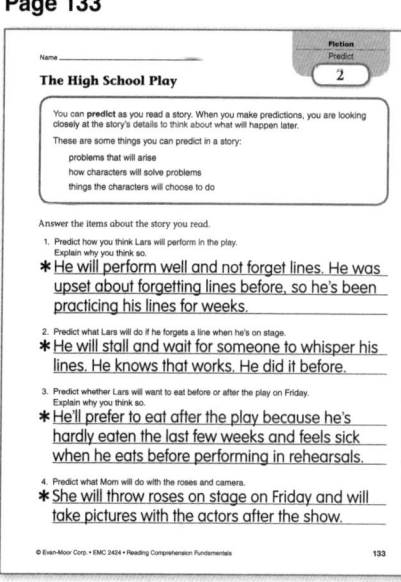

These answers will vary. Examples are given.

Page 134
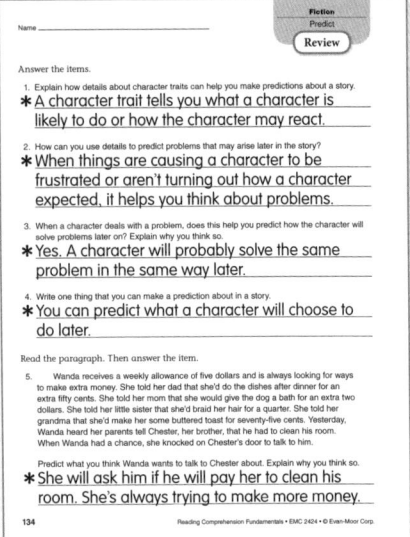

Page 135
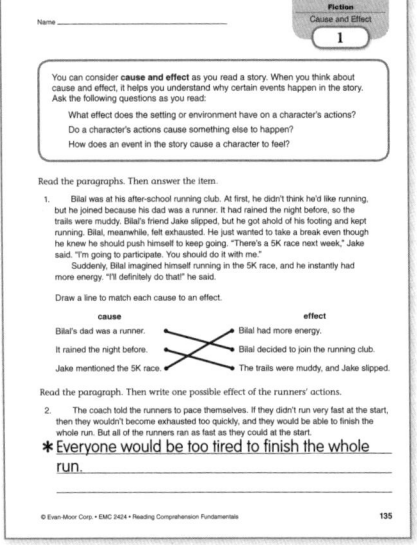

Page 137
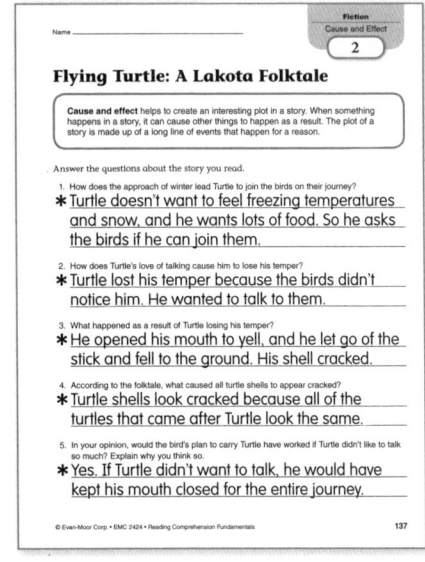

Page 138
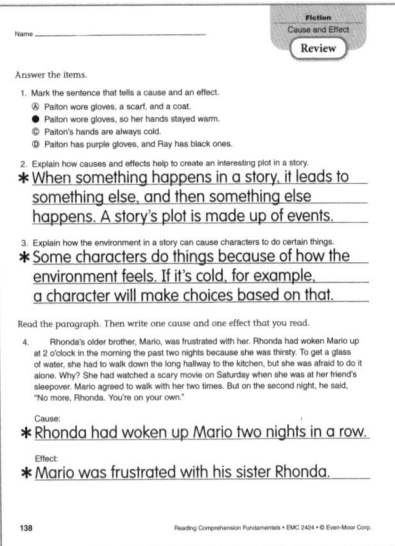

Page 139
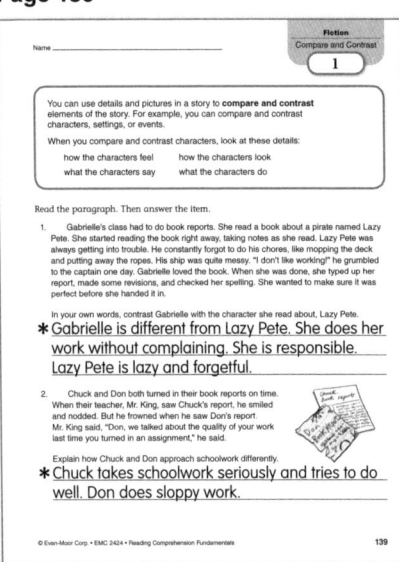

Page 141
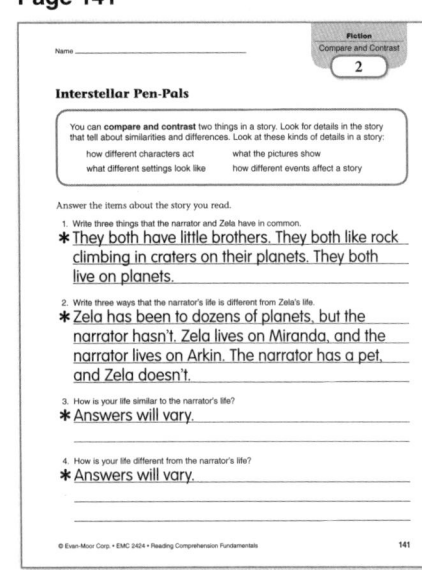

Page 142
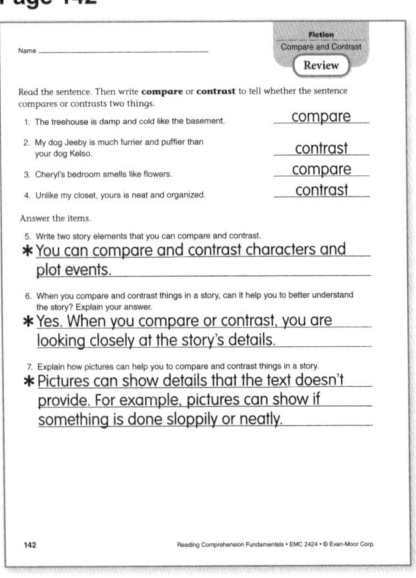

Page 143
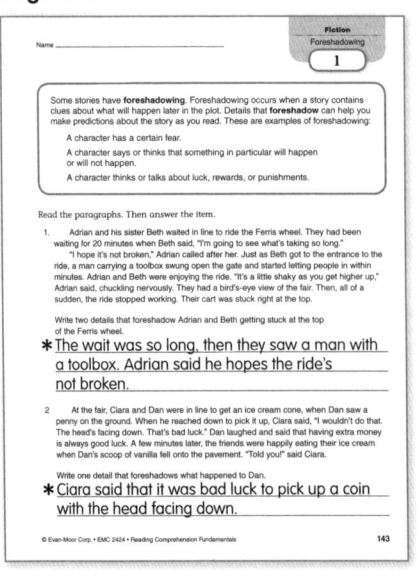

Page 145
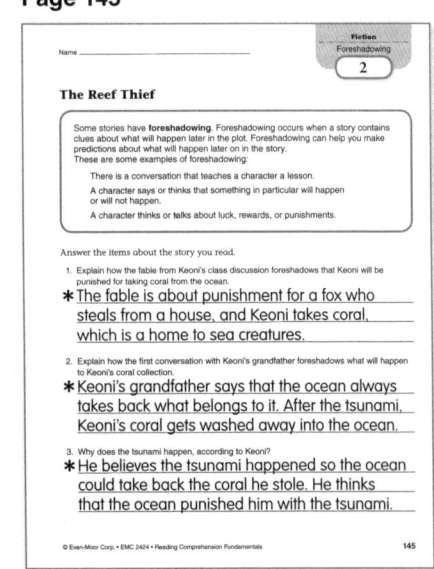

These answers will vary. Examples are given.

Page 146
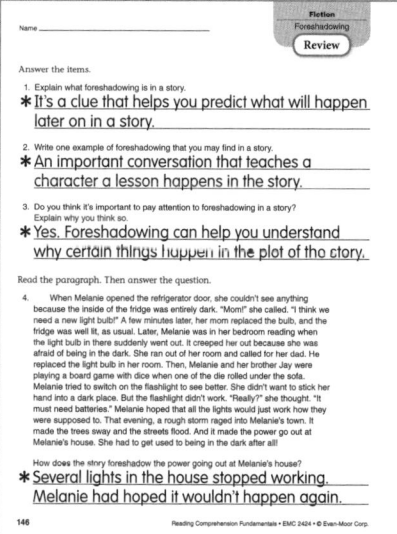

1. Explain what foreshadowing is in a story.
   * It's a clue that helps you predict what will happen later on in a story.
2. Write one example of foreshadowing that you may find in a story.
   * An important conversation that teaches a character a lesson happens in the story.
3. Do you think it's important to pay attention to foreshadowing? Explain why you think so.
   * Yes. Foreshadowing can help you understand why certain things happen in the plot of the story.
4. How does the story foreshadow the power going out at Melanie's house?
   * Several lights in the house stopped working. Melanie had hoped it wouldn't happen again.

Page 147
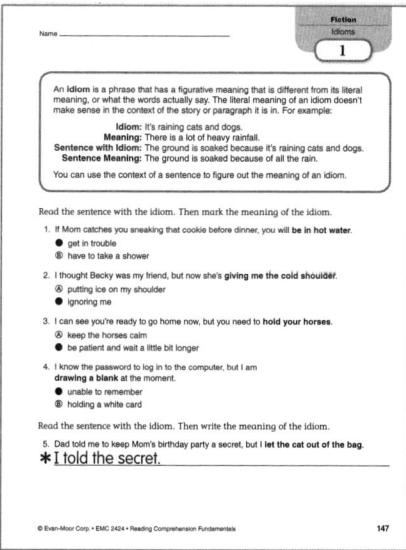

1. be in hot water — get in trouble
2. giving me the cold shoulder — ignoring me
3. hold your horses — be patient and wait a little bit longer
4. drawing a blank at the moment — unable to remember
5. let the cat out of the bag.
   * I told the secret.

Page 149
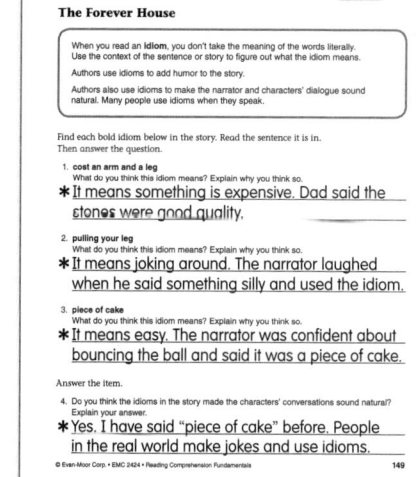

The Forever House

1. cost an arm and a leg
   * It means something is expensive. Dad said the stones were good quality.
2. pulling your leg
   * It means joking around. The narrator laughed when he said something silly and used the idiom.
3. piece of cake
   * It means easy. The narrator was confident about bouncing the ball and said it was a piece of cake.
4. Do you think the idioms in the story made the characters' conversations sound natural? Explain your answer.
   * Yes. I have said "piece of cake" before. People in the real world make jokes and use idioms.

Page 150
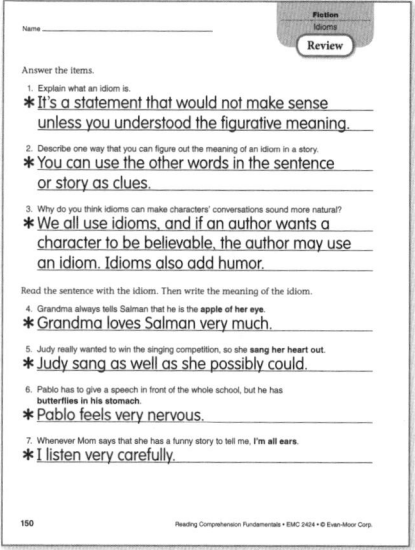

1. Explain what an idiom is.
   * It's a statement that would not make sense unless you understood the figurative meaning.
2. Describe one way that you can figure out the meaning of an idiom in a story.
   * You can use the other words in the sentence or story as clues.
3. Why do you think idioms can make characters' conversations sound more natural?
   * We all use idioms, and if an author wants a character to be believable, the author may use an idiom. Idioms also add humor.
4. Grandma always tells Salman that he is the apple of her eye.
   * Grandma loves Salman very much.
5. Judy really wanted to win the singing competition, so she sang her heart out.
   * Judy sang as well as she possibly could.
6. Pablo has to give a speech in front of the whole school, but he has butterflies in his stomach.
   * Pablo feels very nervous.
7. Whenever Mom says that she has a funny story to tell me, I'm all ears.
   * I listen very carefully.

Page 151
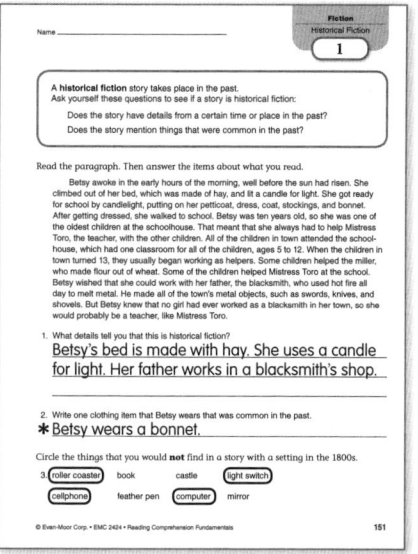

1. What details tell you that this is historical fiction?
   * Betsy's bed is made with hay. She uses a candle for light. Her father works in a blacksmith's shop.
2. Write one clothing item that Betsy wears that was common in the past.
   * Betsy wears a bonnet.
3. Circled: roller coaster, cellphone, light switch, computer

Page 153
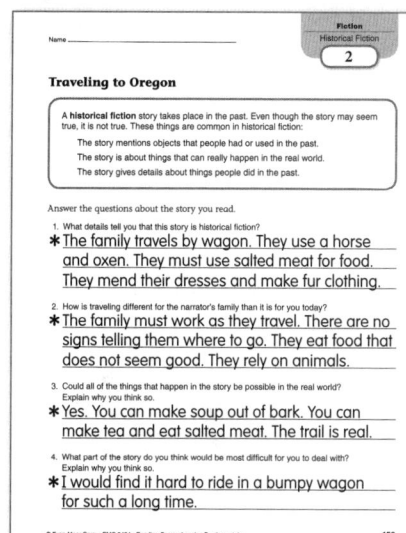

Traveling to Oregon

1. What details tell you that this story is historical fiction?
   * The family travels by wagon. They use a horse and oxen. They must use salted meat for food. They mend their dresses and make fur clothing.
2. How is traveling different for the narrator's family than it is for you today?
   * The family must work as they travel. There are no signs telling them where to go. They eat food that does not seem good. They rely on animals.
3. Could all of the things that happen in the story be possible in the real world? Explain why you think so.
   * Yes. You can make soup out of bark. You can make tea and eat salted meat. The trail is real.
4. What part of the story do you think would be most difficult for you to deal with? Explain why you think so.
   * I would find it hard to ride in a bumpy wagon for such a long time.

Page 154
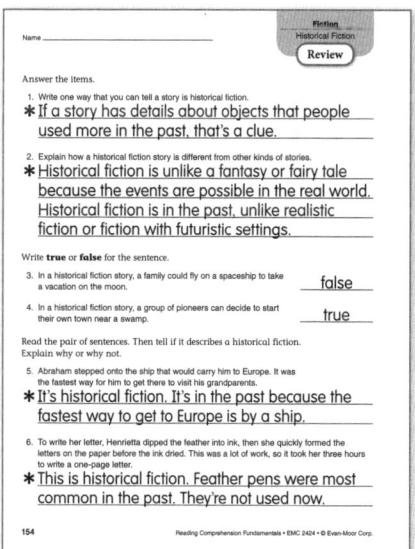

1. Write one way that you can tell a story is historical fiction.
   * If a story has details about objects that people used more in the past, that's a clue.
2. Explain how a historical fiction story is different from other kinds of stories.
   * Historical fiction is unlike a fantasy or fairy tale because the events are possible in the real world. Historical fiction is in the past, unlike realistic fiction or fiction with futuristic settings.
3. false
4. true
5. Abraham stepped onto the ship that would carry him to Europe. It was the fastest way for him to visit his grandparents.
   * It's historical fiction. It's in the past because the fastest way to get to Europe is by ship.
6. To write her letter, Henrietta dipped the feather into ink, then she quickly formed the letters on the paper before the ink dried. This was a lot of work, so it took her three hours to write a one-page letter.
   * This is historical fiction. Feather pens were most common in the past. They're not used now.

Page 155
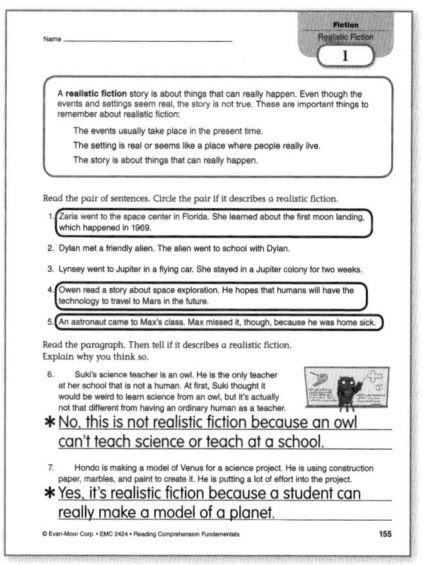

Circled: 1, 4
4. Owen read a story about space exploration. He hopes that humans will have the technology to travel to Mars in the future.
5. An astronaut came to Max's class. Max missed it, though, because he was home sick.

6. Suki's science teacher is an owl...
   * No, this is not realistic fiction because an owl can't teach science or teach at a school.
7. Hondo is making a model of Venus for a science project...
   * Yes, it's realistic fiction because a student can really make a model of a planet.

Page 157
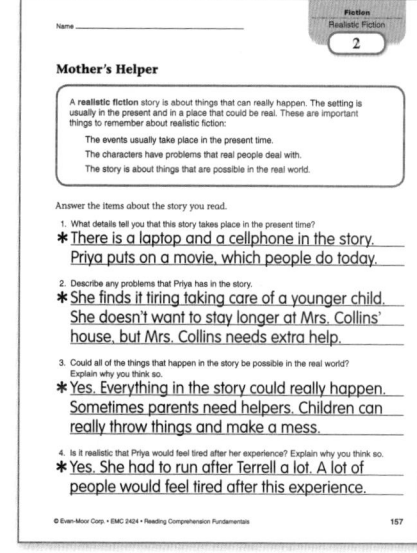

Mother's Helper

1. What details tell you that this story takes place in the present time?
   * There is a laptop and a cellphone in the story. Priya puts on a movie, which people do today.
2. Describe any problems that Priya has in the story.
   * She finds it tiring taking care of a younger child. She doesn't want to stay longer at Mrs. Collins' house, but Mrs. Collins needs extra help.
3. Could all of the things that happen in the story be possible in the real world? Explain why you think so.
   * Yes. Everything in the story could really happen. Sometimes parents need helpers. Children can really throw things and make a mess.
4. Is it realistic that Priya would feel tired after her experience? Explain why you think so.
   * Yes. She had to run after Terrell a lot. A lot of people would feel tired after this experience.

✱ These answers will vary. Examples are given.

Page 158
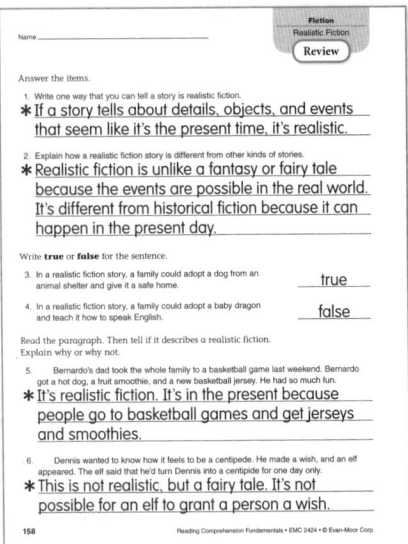

Page 159
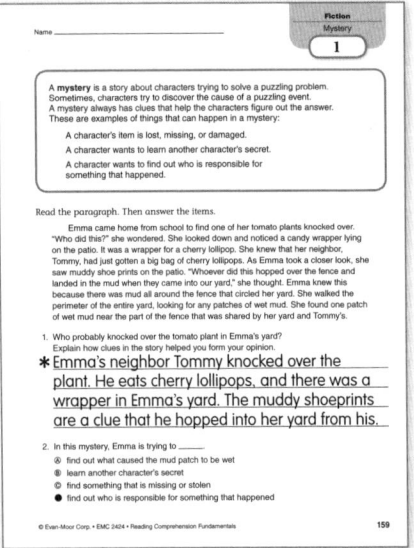

Page 161
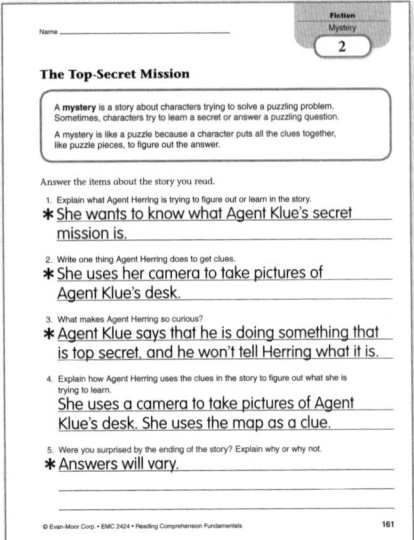

Page 162
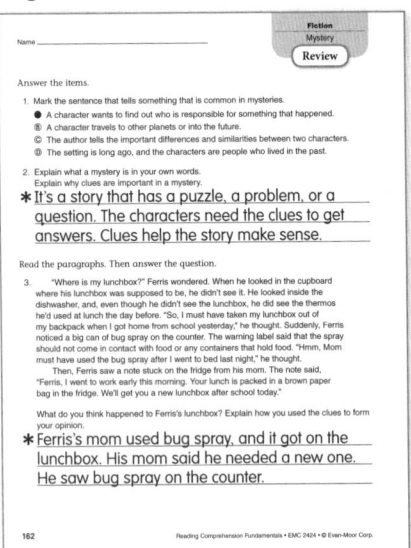